TEACHING TECHNIQUES IN ENGLISH AS A SECOND LANGUAGE
Series Editors: Russell N. Campbell and William E. Rutherford

TECHNIQUES AND RESOURCES IN TEACHING READING

Sandra Silberstein

• OXFORD UNIVERSITY PRESS •

Oxford University Press

200 Madison Avenue
New York, NY 10016 USA

Walton Street
Oxford OX2 6DP England

OXFORD is a trademark of Oxford University Press.

Library of Congress Cataloging-in-Publication Data

Silberstein, Sandra, 1948–
    Techniques and resources in teaching reading / Sandra Silberstein.
      p. cm.—(Teaching techniques in English as a second
language)
    Includes bibliographical references.
    ISBN 0-19-434134-8
    1. English language—Study and teaching—Foreign speakers.
2. Reading.   I. Title.   II. Series.
PE1128.A2S58   1993
428'.007—dc20

ISBN 0-19-434134-8 (pbk.)

·ACKNOWLEDGMENTS·

The following are unindictable for any shortcomings of this volume remaining after their valuable commentary on earlier drafts: Mark A. Clarke (University of Colorado at Denver), David P. Harris (Georgetown University), Margot Haynes (Delta College), Margot Gramer (Oxford University Press), and series editors, Russell Campbell and William Rutherford. Sincere thanks to you all, especially to Mark A. Clarke for twenty years of sapient and whimsical shop talk.

·EDITORS' PREFACE·

It has been apparent for some time that little attention has been given to the needs of practicing and student teachers of English as a Second Language.* Although numerous in-service and pre-service teacher-training programs are offered throughout the world, these often suffer for lack of appropriate instructional materials. Seldom are books written that present practical information that relates directly to daily classroom instruction. What teachers want are useful ideas, suggestions, demonstrations, and examples of teaching techniques that are consistent with established theoretical principles and that others in our profession have found to be expedient, practical, and relevant to the real-life circumstances in which most teachers work.

It was in recognition of this need that we began our search for scholars in our field who had distinguished themselves in particular instructional aspects of second language teaching. We sought out those who had been especially successful in communicating to their colleagues the characteristics of language teaching and testing techniques that have been found to be appropriate for students from elementary school through college and adult education programs. We also sought in those same scholars evidence of an awareness and understanding of current theories of language learning together with the ability to translate the essence of a theory into practical applications for the classroom.

Our search has been successful. For this volume, as well as for others in this series, we have chosen a colleague who is extraordinarily competent and exceedingly willing to share with practicing teachers the considerable knowledge that she has gained from many years of experience.

---

*In this volume, and in others in the series, we have chosen to use *English as a Second Language (ESL)* to refer to English teaching in the United States (as a second language) *as well as* English in other countries (as a foreign language).

Professor Silberstein's book is devoted entirely to the presentation and exemplification of practical techniques in the teaching of reading. Each chapter of her book contains, in addition to detailed consideration of a wide variety of techniques, a number of activities that teachers can perform that tie the content of the book directly to the teachers' responsibilities in their classes. With this volume then, a critical need in the language teaching field has been met.

We are extremely pleased to join with the authors in this series and with Oxford University Press in making these books available to our fellow teachers. We are confident that the books will enable language teachers around the world to increase their effectiveness while at the same time making their task an easier and more enjoyable one.

Russell N. Campbell
William E. Rutherford

To Mother,
Maia,
and Doug;
in memory of my father

·CONTENTS·

Introduction · **xii**

Chapter One · **Introduction to Second Language Reading** · 3

Chapter Two · **Teaching as Decision Making** · 15

Chapter Three · **Nonprose Reading** · 19

Chapter Four · **Expository Prose** · 43

Chapter Five · **Editorializing and Opinion** · 74

Chapter Six · **Fiction, Poetry, and Songs** · 88

Chapter Seven · **Developing Instructional Materials** · 101

Bibliography · 115

Index · 121

·INTRODUCTION·

Current models of the reading process focus on the interactive relation of reader and text. From this perspective, reading is understood to be a complex cognitive process in which reader and text interact to (re)create meaningful discourse. Like contemporary reading theory, this book puts text and reader at its center; it is organized around the types of texts typically encountered by adolescent and adult students of English already literate in their first languages.

Obviously, no book about teaching techniques can furnish a set of recipes to be followed without reflection. Accordingly, this volume presents practical suggestions both for instructional activities and for evaluating the ongoing life of the classroom.

The introductory chapter comprises an overview of the reading process, illustrated by a "visit" to a reading class. Although it is obviously impossible to capture a "real" classroom experience on paper, the goal is to provide readers with a sense of the life of the classroom and of the decisions with which teachers and students are faced. Succeeding chapters survey diverse classrooms and students through the presentation of sample lessons; these are followed by lists of additional activities appropriate to the text type.

The second chapter comprises a discussion of teaching as a decision-making enterprise. The issues raised in this short chapter are fundamental to the rest of the book. The students and texts represented in the sample lessons (beginning in Chapter Three) are diverse. The third chapter introduces nonprose reading in the contexts of classes in both survival English and English for academic purposes. Chapter Four considers expository prose found in academic settings, while Chapter Five uses a science text to introduce the concepts of editorializing and opinion. Both of these contexts invite a content-centered approach to reading.[1] In Chapter Six, we encounter literature and songs in an intensive English language center whose curriculum allows for both integrated skills instruction and individualized, extensive reading.

Sample lessons are followed by examples intended for different settings and proficiency levels. Illustrations from a wide variety of sources demonstrate the types of materials available. Grounded in a teacher's systematic perspective on reading, these activities can be adapted to a variety of contexts. The last chapter provides an overview for teachers interested in developing their own instructional materials. Each chapter ends with an Activities section to encourage further exploration of concepts and techniques. Notes are provided to facilitate further reading.

By design, this book does not advocate a single classroom format. The activities presented will prove appropriate to a variety of curricular formats from completely integrated so-called whole language, task-based, or experiential classrooms,[2] to those whose sole purpose is the improvement of reading skills. Nonetheless, the varied classroom descriptions share certain characteristics. In each instance, teacher intervention is minimized. Our premise is that individual readers approach particular texts with specific objectives. Instructors adopt a facilitating role: locating texts suited to students' goals and interests and introducing techniques appropriate to the task at hand. Teachers participate in discussions on an equal footing, acknowledging student expertise in content areas.

In this instructional context, the chapters that follow examine techniques and resources in teaching reading from the perspective of reader and text.

Seattle, Washington   Sandra Silberstein
1994

Notes

[1]For further discussion of content-centered classrooms, see Mohan (1986).
[2]For further discussion on the topic of whole language classrooms, see Edelsky, Altwerger & Flores (1991); Goodman (1986); and Rigg (1991). For discussions of communicative task-based classrooms, see Nunan (1989, 1991). Legutke & Thomas (1991) discuss communicative tasks within an experiential view of learning.

TECHNIQUES
AND
RESOURCES
IN
TEACHING
READING

CHAPTER ONE

INTRODUCTION TO SECOND LANGUAGE READING

AN ENGLISH LANGUAGE CLASS

This is Just to Say

I have eaten
the plums
that were in

the icebox
and which
you were probably
saving
for breakfast

Forgive me
they were delicious

so sweet and
so cold.

William Carlos Williams

We are in an ESOL class in an intensive English center of the sort widespread in English-speaking countries. This is a heterogeneous group— twelve students, two each from Japan and Saudi Arabia; one each from Argentina, Brazil, China, Egypt, Germany, Kuwait, Mexico, and Thailand. This intermediate-level class meets daily for one hour.

The group has been discussing an article on attitudes toward the arts. The article claims that the average undergraduate may encounter no poetry during the course of a liberal arts education and documents the decreased government funding of the arts. Reactions to the article are mixed. A number of students insist that the author is correct. They have noticed that artists are not revered in their host country as they are in their home countries. Some have read Shakespeare and are disappointed that English-speaking students show little interest in their English language heritage. Others say simply that the world is changing: These students no longer read their own traditional literature; many are more interested in engineering.

A student from Saudi Arabia says with passion, "A country cannot live without its literature." Several students nod in agreement. A student from Japan adds, "My roommate says he has never read a poem. Can this be true?" Until now, the students have been speaking to each other. All eyes turn to the instructor. Before she can respond, another student adds, "I have never read a poem in English." Several students agree that they would like to read a short poem. Before the bell rings, the class agrees that each student will ask English-speaking roommates or friends about their attitudes toward poetry. They will report their findings in three days. The teacher's assignment is to bring a poem to class.

When students enter the next day, the poem is already on the board. They sit in a semicircle, quietly reading. A student teacher sits among them. "Is this a poem?" a student asks. "Some people think this is a lovely poem," responds the teacher, "but others don't think it is a poem at all." "Yes, my roommate says all poetry must rhyme," offers the Brazilian student. "It looks like haiku," observes a Japanese student approvingly. "What is the poem about?" asks another student. "This is the question," the instructor agrees. She reads the poem aloud slowly:

This is Just to Say

I have eaten
the plums
that were in

the icebox
and which
you were probably
saving
for breakfast

Forgive me
they were delicious

so sweet and
so cold.

William Carlos Williams

There is silence. As the teacher wonders whether to repeat the question, the student from Kuwait offers, "This is a note." "It looks like a poem," says another student. "But it sounds like a note," the Kuwaiti explains.

Again there is silence. "But a poem is never what it seems," contributes the student from Thailand. Many heads nod. "Hidden meaning," whispers one student to herself. She smiles at the teacher. Several students repeat, "Hidden meaning."

Students are silent as they reread the poem looking for something beneath the obvious. "It looks like a note," agrees the student from Mexico. "The person is sorry because he ate the plums. The person writes, 'Forgive me.' " " 'Forgive me' seems too polite. Do you say 'forgive me'?" asks the Egyptian student of the teacher. "It is somewhat formal or serious," the instructor agrees.

Suddenly the student from Argentina is animated: "This is a letter. Why does it not say 'Dear William'?" "This is not a letter, it is a note," counters one of his classmates. "Yes?" He is not persuaded. "Well, maybe the person knows the other person very well," explains his classmate. "They live in the same house," contributes a student from Saudi Arabia. "Maybe they are sisters," offers a Japanese student. "No, they are husband and wife, or lovers," counters the German. "Maybe brothers," offers another. Eyes turn toward the instructor, hoping for mediation. "But what is the poem about?" she asks once again. "Hidden meaning," repeats a student.

There is silence again as the students reread the poem to themselves. They begin to look carefully at the language: "This word *just*, does it mean *only?*" The Chinese student has turned to the student teacher sitting nearby. She wants some confirmation from a native speaker. "I've been thinking about this, too," he responds with a twinkle in his eye. "When people say *just* to me, I think they mean just the opposite: like when a salesperson says to me, 'I don't mean to say that you're fat, I just think you should try a larger size!' " Everyone laughs. Class members suspend their concentration as they take a few moments to shift in their seats.

The Egyptian student brings the class back into focus. "So this is not just a note?" "It asks for forgiveness," says another student. "He ate the plums, he says, 'forgive me.' " "But the person will not be angry, really," a Saudi Arabian student observes. "Maybe he just wants to say the plums are wonderful," adds his Mexican classmate. "The person is not angry, so he just says thank you for the delicious plums."

"I think it is a love letter," the German student proposes. Other students begin to agree. "The writer shares a delicious experience," offers the Kuwaiti student. "It is a love letter between two sisters who live together," volunteers a Japanese student. "Two sisters cannot write a love letter," the German student responds. "Yes they can," chorus the Thai and Japanese students. The bell rings.

PERSPECTIVES ON THE READING PROCESS

This composite of many actual class discussions illustrates a number of aspects of reading theory. We first notice that reading is an active process. The students worked intensively, interacting with the text in order to create meaningful discourse. Although reading has sometimes been characterized as "passive" or "receptive," as early as 1917, Thorndike (cited in Venezky, 1984) established the notion that reading is an active process related to problem solving. More recently, scholars (notably Goodman, 1967, and Smith, 1971) developed a **psycholinguistic** perspective of reading, focusing on its active, cognitive processes. According to this point of view, efficient readers develop predictions about the content of a passage. Along with textual clues, knowledge and experience help readers develop expectations about what they will read. The efficient reader then reads rapidly to confirm or refute these predictions. If hypotheses are confirmed, the reader continues with an increasing store of information on the topic. If they are not confirmed, the reader returns and rereads more carefully.

The psycholinguistic model of reading described sampling and guessing of vocabulary and syntax, a facet that has recently been challenged (see Grabe, 1991). However, the concept of hypothesis formation remains important. The students described above approached their task with prior knowledge about poems: what they mean and how they are to be read. Students' expectations were triggered by the fact that the passage looked like a poem and was presented as such by their teacher. They recognized that the abbreviated language of poetry invites the reader to explore relationships that are not made explicit. Thus, students mistrusted an initial reading that suggested the text was no more than a note. Their expectation that poetic meaning transcend the mundane had not been confirmed; the students reread.

Contemporary Interactive Perspectives

Interactive approaches to reading have focused on two concepts of interaction.[1] First is the interaction of two types of cognitive skills that Grabe (1991) terms identification and interpretation. Fluent readers seem to simultaneously employ what have come to be known as **lower**

level skills that allow them to rapidly and automatically recognize words (and presumably grammatical forms), while **higher level skills** allow them to comprehend and interpret. Lower level skills involve rapid and precise unconscious processing (**automaticity**).[2] In the class we observed, we can assume that students were already relatively efficient at lower level processing. Their problems lay primarily with the second aspect of interactive reading: interaction between reader and text.

In contemporary approaches to reading, meaning is not seen as being fully present in a text waiting to be decoded. Rather, meaning is created through the interaction of reader and text.

Schema Theory

Reader expectations are based on readers' prior knowledge. Background knowledge that aids in text comprehension has recently been studied under the rubric of **schema theory**. This theoretical framework (aptly termed by Grabe, 1991, a "theoretical metaphor") emphasizes the role of preexisting knowledge (a reader's "schemata") in providing the reader with information that is implicit in a text.[3] In the class described above, students relied on their "poetry schemata" for information about how poems look and mean. One might also say that they relied on their "intimacy schemata" to determine the relationship between the interlocutors represented in the poem.

From this perspective, text comprehension requires the simultaneous interaction of two modes of information processing. **Bottom-up** (or **text-based**) processing occurs when linguistic input from the text is mapped against the reader's previous knowledge. This process is also termed **data driven** because it is evoked by the incoming data. Students relied on text-based processing as they returned to the poem to read and reread, calling attention to specific sections of the text. Bottom-up reading requires language processing at all levels: word, sentence, and discourse.

Top-down, knowledge-based, or **conceptually driven** information processing occurs when readers use prior knowledge to make predictions about the data they will find in a text. Activities that assist students in gaining or accessing background knowledge facilitate top-down processing. In the class described above, students' knowledge of poetry, based on previous reading and experience, was supplemented and activated through a prereading discussion. Formats typically suggested to develop top-down processing skills include reading within a topic area (**content-centered instruction**) and **extensive reading**

or **sustained silent reading (SSR),** in which students read large amounts of text for general comprehension. This latter approach is discussed in Chapter Six. Successful reading requires skill in both top-down and bottom-up processing.

Two kinds of background knowledge—**formal schemata,** involving knowledge of rhetorical structures and conventions, and **content schemata,** involving knowledge of the world beyond texts— provide us with explanations for students who "misread" the poem as communication between siblings. These students applied culturally divergent intimacy schemata either for rhetorical conventions or for actual relationships. They did not perceive the poem as an example of intimate discourse, nor did they recognize what many would see as a poetic convention of sensuality in the description of the plums: "so sweet and so cold." Moreover, the content of the poem did not match these students' notions of communication between lovers.[4]

Schemata are accessed and expectations developed, in part, through context. Beginning this chapter, readers may have been perplexed to confront a poem with no introduction. Unfortunately, one too seldom finds discussions of poetry in the field of TESOL. Initially experiencing the poem without immediate or prior context, readers may have wondered if they had misunderstood the intent of this book. ESOL students who are given no context in which to read culturally unfamiliar discourse may find themselves similarly bewildered. They approach the text without relevant schemata and with few hunches about its content; they will find it difficult to judge if hypotheses have been confirmed.

A word of caution is in order, however, concerning the implications of schema theory for second language reading instruction. Given the fundamental role of preexisting knowledge in the comprehending process, one might assume that students can therefore read only about what they know. This is not the case. It would be a disservice to rob students of the opportunity to learn through reading. Similarly, it is not necessary or desirable for teachers to prepare students for everything they will encounter in texts. Along with information about texts and language, students need only a reasonable context and some knowledge of the topic to begin to learn from reading.

Notice that in our sample class, the poem was read in the context of a student-generated discussion, supplemented by the teacher's observation that the poem represents a break with some elements of the cultural tradition.

By reminding students that one reads first to see what a passage is about, the instructor helped students set goals for an initial reading and called attention to the skills and strategies that might serve them best. Knowledge of cognition (**metacognition**) and the ability to monitor one's comprehending processes can aid in successful reading (for an overview, see Grabe, 1991). Developing metacognitive awareness is an appropriate goal of a reading curriculum.

Interactive Reading Theories in the Humanities and Humanistic Social Sciences

The challenge posed by the Williams poem, or any text, is the creation of meaning: Reading is a communicative activity. Current approaches to texts in diverse disciplines stress the interactive nature of what Cicourel (1974, p. 40) calls "interpretive procedures."[5] Like the other perspectives we have examined, these approaches assume that meaning is created through the interaction of text and interlocutor.

Literary theorists note that authorial intent can never be completely recovered by a reader. Nor can authors completely represent their intent. Thus, readers have the task of incompletely recovering a message that has been incompletely coded. Lest one despair of the utility of reading at all, Widdowson (1979) observes:

> I think the inaccessibility of intentions has been somewhat exaggerated. The writer of a particular instance of discourse may have individual intentions, but he [or she] has to convey these through certain conventions which define the kind of discourse he [or she] is producing. If conventions did not exist to mediate the communication between writer and reader, then intentions could not be conveyed at all. (p. 165)

This issue of intention and meaning will become central after the bell has rung. Students will want to know if the Williams poem was written to a partner or a sibling. The instructor may judge it pedantic to elaborate poetic conventions of intimacy. She may well want to stress the "correctness" of either interpretation. After all, one might say that this poem displays and celebrates intimacy. Either interpretation recognizes the basic conventions of intimate discourse in English. After several false starts, all students confirmed some expectations concerning poetic conventions of intimacy and human relations. Students thus proved to be independent, successful readers. There would seem to be little need to precisely confirm authorial intent.

As teachers, we may find it useful to note that the details of "schemata" for intimate discourse will differ cross-culturally, thus explaining the spouse/sibling debate. Divergent schemata also explain another unexpected student response. Students' schema for poetry described as "hidden meaning" assumes an invisible, symbolic level of interpretation eschewed by contemporary non-Freudian critical theory. Current approaches seek, instead, to recover what remains implicit in the text. Interesting as these observations may be for the teacher, they are not essential for the students. The interpretive procedures used by these readers proved effective. Is it appropriate, then, to invoke schemata to judge some of their readings "incorrect"?

This is the dilemma faced by the instructor at the moment of the bell. By declining to reveal "the answer," she reinforces the role of the independent reader. Alternatively, she may elect to broaden students' acquaintance with poetry schemata and conventions of intimacy. It will require discipline to implement the first option. As a writer, I can easily refuse to reveal the relationship of Williams to his addressee. Withholding information is more difficult to accomplish face-to-face.

The Role of the Reading Teacher

Had the teacher seen herself principally as an arbiter and authority, few such dilemmas would arise. This expedient, however, cannot foster independence in language learners:

> It becomes the responsibility of the teacher to train students to determine their own goals and strategies for a particular reading ... to encourage students to take risks, to guess, to ignore their impulses to be always correct. (Clarke & Silberstein, 1977, p. 135)

Notice that the teacher described above was an expert only in language issues; like each member of the class, she had specific areas of expertise to contribute. Her goal was to create an environment of independent, problem-solving readers who chose what to read and who practiced strategies for efficient reading. Students initiated the introduction of poetry into the classroom. They recognized the importance of setting goals for a reading task and of using appropriate strategies to achieve those goals. (The teacher had presumably worked on issues of metacognitive awareness at an earlier stage.) Here, the teacher's role was facilitative. Ironically, the goal of language teachers is to make themselves dispensable. The contradictions and difficulties inherent in this task are the province of the chapter that follows.

Activities in the Reading Class

If students are to become independent language users, they will need to experience a range of reading tasks corresponding to the kinds of reading they intend in the target language. Silberstein (1974) and Widdowson (1974, 1975) argue that comprehension of poetry requires the same interpretive processes required for any text. Our sample class demonstrates the use of procedures appropriate for many kinds of reading. As would be the case with many texts, students first **skimmed** the poem to obtain a general sense of its content. One often skims, for example, to determine if a more careful reading is warranted.

This initial reading was followed by a more careful examination of the poem. More detailed **reading for thorough comprehension** allowed students to paraphrase the author's ideas: "He ate the plums, he says 'forgive me.' " Unfortunately, the literal restatement of a text is the sole focus of many reading activities. In this instance, the students went further. Some **scanned**, looking for specific words or phrases (that they had previously recognized automatically) that would support their arguments. Through **critical reading** students drew inferences and recognized implicit relationships, which allowed them finally to create a meaningful discourse. Students returned to the text using different strategies to achieve comprehension. Only through this multiple approach did meaning emerge. Students had learned to define comprehension in terms of this multiple/critical approach to texts.

The poem proved realistic both in terms of communicative language use and student abilities. As with all reading, the passage and its context suggested appropriate reading tasks. One need only consider the monotonous parallelism of most textbook exercises to appreciate the import of this observation. If students are to be encouraged to fit reading strategies to text, teachers must not demand the same activities for each reading passage. Individual texts will suggest particular teaching activities. A passage written largely in the passive voice, for example, "cries out" for work on the passive, *but* only if the passive constructions are instrumental to comprehension. Similarly, one would not encourage students to undertake a careful syntactic analysis of a passage that merited only rapid scanning for a single piece of information. The format of "This is Just to Say," along with its contextual presentation, suggested that students consider cultural definitions of poetry. As some native speakers consider this marvelous poetry, students were invited to go beyond the format of a note to find the intimacy of the poem. Meaning was created through the interaction of students and text.

SUMMARY

In this chapter we have reviewed fundamental principles of reading theory. Aspects of the reading process can be usefully summarized within the rubric presented by Grabe (1991):

Automatic recognition skills. Readers need to be able to automatically identify words and grammatical forms.

Vocabulary and structural knowledge. Fluent readers possess a large receptive vocabulary and knowledge of syntactic and rhetorical structure. Obviously these are acquired through the act of reading. Formal instruction in language structure is reviewed in Chapter Four; vocabulary instruction is addressed in Chapter Seven.

Content and background knowledge. Our poetry lesson demonstrated the importance of text-related and cultural knowledge to the comprehension of texts. Such knowledge needs to be provided or accessed if students are to read texts effectively.

Synthesis and evaluation skills and strategies formed the basis of much of the activity we encountered in our sample lesson. Students synthesized information and anticipated the author's perspective. Through these processes, students compared textual information with prior knowledge to evaluate the poem.

Metacognitive knowledge and skills monitoring. Students were aware of their goals and their choices of strategies to achieve these. They recognized discourse patterns of poetry and adjusted their strategies when they became dissatisfied with a current interpretation.

The balance of this volume addresses the last four elements of the reading process.[6] In succeeding chapters, sample lessons and activities will assume the following perspectives:

Reading is a complex information processing skill in which the reader interacts with text in order to (re)create meaningful discourse.

The reader is an active, problem-solving individual who coordinates a number of skills and strategies to facilitate comprehension.

The goal of a reading program is to develop fluent, independent readers who set their own goals and strategies for reading. Students learn aspects of the reading process through reading.

Reading activities are suggested by the goals of the readers and by specific characteristics of the reading passage. Reading tasks must be realistic in terms of both language use and students' abilities.

·ACTIVITIES·

1. Consider some of the implications of current reading theory.
   a. Some of current second language reading theory is based on first language research. What are differences between learning to read in a native versus a target language? What are the advantages that second language readers bring to the task?
   b. Carrell (1987) notes that efficient readers rely on both text-based and knowledge-based information processing. What kinds of problems face readers who rely too heavily on either of these?
2. Apply current reading theory.
   a. Choose a short poem that would be appropriate for a group of students with whom you work (or feel free to define a hypo-thetical group). What characteristics make this poem appropriate for your students? In what context would it be read? In broad terms, what would be the format of a class session using this poem?
   b. Examine how you read a second language. Choose a text on a topic with which you are familiar and that is appropriate to your proficiency level. Determine appropriate goals and read. Reflect on the experience in the context of current reading theory.
   c. Consider the sample lesson: What should the instructor do when the bell rings?

Notes

[1]For an excellent overview of current reading research and theory, see Grabe (1991).
[2]There have been a number of suggestions for developing automaticity. Stoller (1986) recommends exercises that increase reading rate and develop rapid recognition and identification. Rate-building exercises generally involve timed activities designed for consciousness-raising. Recognition activities tend to involve columns of words and of phrases that must be read rapidly in order to determine if columns are the same or different, or to identify the item that is incongruous. In contrast, Nagy and Herman (1987) recommend extensive reading to improve automaticity.

³For an introduction to schema theory, see Adams and Collins (1979); Carrell and
Eisterhold (1983); and Rumelhart (1980). For a discussion of schema theory in the
context of related interactive perspectives, see Grabe (1988, 1991).

⁴Carrell (1987) presents a useful discussion of the interaction of content and formal
schemata.

⁵For a broader view of approaches to text in various disciplines, the following contain
useful discussions: In literary theory, see, for example, Belsey (1980); Eagleton
(1984); Fetterly (1978); Flynn (1986); Rosenblat (1978); and Tompkins (1980).
In film theory, see, for example, de Lauretis (1984); Minh-ha (1989, 1991); and
Mulvey (1989). In anthropology, see, for example, Clifford and Marcus (1986).

⁶See Stoller (1986) for suggestions for setting up a reading lab to develop automaticity.
For additional suggestions, see Eskey and Grabe (1988); Gatbonton and Segalowitz
(1988); Herman (1985); Nagy and Herman (1987); and Samuels (1979).

·CHAPTER TWO·

TEACHING AS DECISION MAKING

Surveying the lesson described in Chapter One, we find many instances of instructor decision making. The teacher was not able to teach by preplanned formula; rather, in the context of her planning, she evaluated the ongoing life of the classroom.

The initial decision to read poetry was suggested by a student-generated exploration of ideas, but the teacher had to decide how to respond to this unexpected direction. She made her decision under the pressure of time at the end of the hour, deciding simultaneously (a) that she would bring poetry to class, (b) when she would bring it, (c) what she would suggest the students do by way of preparation.

Along with the careful thought and planning that teachers bring to a classroom, this type of rapid decision making characterizes the teaching process. Throughout the subsequent class hour, the teacher had to decide whether and how to repeat or rephrase questions, when to supply further information or summary, and whether and how to respond to student queries. We all make a seemingly infinite number of these decisions during each hour that we teach. As we sit silently listening to our students, we are listening to more than what they actually say. We are also observing silent students to see if they have understood their peers and to see if they seem to need help in gaining the floor. We are noting whether a discussion seems to call for additional information or focus, whether a topic has exhausted itself, or whether a student response suggests a new direction or an entrance into observations that we have wanted to make. To be sure, there are many different kinds of classrooms, ranging from those whose activities are largely prescribed by teachers and administrators to those that seek almost complete student autonomy. In almost all instances, however, the teacher makes decisions moment-by-moment, determining how to respond to student needs and queries.

In the context of trying to encourage student autonomy, the typical instructor must also juggle the often contradictory demands of limited time, institutionalized curricula, student expectations, and individual student needs.

There is no simple recipe by which one can always teach reading to all students. Some students benefit from more intervention in the reading process than do others (Krashen & Terrell, 1983). Some, for example, enjoy risk taking, while other students require a good deal of encouragement. Some benefit from explicit instruction in reading strategies more than do others.[1] Notwithstanding this diversity, it is possible for teachers to make principled decisions about reading instruction derived from systematic questioning of the teaching context.

A. Looking at their *students,* teachers can ask themselves the following questions:

1. What kind of reading will the students need to do in English?
- Our goal is to emphasize the kinds of tasks students will encounter in English. Generally, this suggests focusing on texts that are similar to students' target texts. However, our poetry lesson demonstrates that a variety of text types can encourage practice in similar approaches to texts.

2. What kinds of texts do the students read in their native language?
- It is helpful to determine if there are strategies and skills that their students already possess in first language reading that teachers can help them transfer to second language tasks.

3. Do class activities help students to become active decision makers and risk takers?
- Activities can be organized to foster independent readers who set their own goals and strategies for reading.

4. Do class activities respond to individual student needs?
- Individual students may require explicit instruction in different aspects of reading: skimming, scanning, understanding organizational clues, accessing prior knowledge, making hypotheses, etc.

B. Looking at *texts,* teachers can ask themselves the following questions:

1. What kind(s) of reading does the text invite?
- The task is to develop activities and contexts that parallel the most realistic and appropriate approaches to a given text. For example, it would not be the best choice for students to read

with great care a text that does not merit close attention outside the reading class.

2. In what respects is this text or the way(s) it can be read similar to the kinds of reading the students will need to do in English?

- Activities can be organized to reflect the kinds of tasks students are most likely to encounter.
- Activities can be organized to reflect the kinds of tasks individual students most need to practice.

Like the teaching process, no discussion of pedagogy can be reduced to a set of formulas to be adopted without reflection. The chapters that follow present a number of contexts in which students read texts. These examples and accompanying discussions demonstrate some of the decisions facing teachers and students. Reflecting on these examples, readers of this volume will determine for themselves the kinds of decisions they will make as they help their students learn to read English.

It is important to note that goals are achieved partially and gradually. It is easy to be daunted by mythical instructors in teacher preparation texts. In Chapter One, our mythical instructor accustomed her students to ask only for language and cultural information unavailable to them. Her self-directed students gave her little cause to direct the discussion, nor to answer her own questions. Moreover, she had created an atmosphere of sufficient trust that each student was willing and able to speak in front of the group, even to disagree when necessary. That completely successful classroom lessons do not exist is worth noting. But only that. This book is about goals. These provide the road map for helping students to become successful readers. There will be digressions along the way. But with map in hand, one continues the journey. The precise itinerary is determined en route by teacher and student.

One final word of encouragement is in order as teachers become independent decision makers and, by definition, researchers of their own classrooms[2]: Just as students need the freedom to take risks as they negotiate texts, teachers must take risks as they negotiate the "tightrope" of language teaching:

> Like the tightrope walker who needs the freedom to be unstable, and thereby remain on the wire, teachers need the slack to make their own decisions, to be wrong on occasion, but to stay on the wire. (Clarke & Silberstein, 1988, pp. 698–699)

·ACTIVITIES·

1. Observe an ESL reading class or a reading session in an integrated language skills program. Note as many instances as you can of teacher decision making. Choose several instances and reflect on (a) the decisions that were made, and (b) the basis on which these decisions might have been made.

2. In the same class, what kinds of decisions did the students make?

3. What are the constraints you experience (or foresee) in your current (or future) teaching situations? In the case of constraints you judge to be particularly negative, are there decisions you can make to ameliorate the situation?

Notes

[1]For discussions of strategy training, see Carrell, Pharis, and Liberto (1989); Grabe (1991); and Chapter Four in this volume.

[2]For an introduction to teachers as researchers, see Allwright and Bailey (1991). Also, for a discussion of teachers as theorists, see Prabhu, (1992).

·CHAPTER THREE·

NONPROSE READING

THE SUNG FAMILY: NONPROSE READING AT DIFFERENT PROFICIENCY LEVELS

The Sung family members are recently arrived immigrants to an English-speaking country. While they are getting settled, the Sungs are staying with a host family. Mr. and Mrs. Sung are anxious to find jobs and to improve their English by attending evening classes. In order to find employment and to purchase second-hand furniture, the Sungs will need to consult the classified advertisements in the local newspaper. They will need to decipher the city bus schedule in order to attend job interviews and English classes. Though the Sungs are considered literate in their own language, they received only a few years of formal education before they were forced to leave school in order to work. Their spoken English is limited. Until now, the Sungs' experience in reading English has been confined to the English advertising logos that permeated the capital city of their homeland.

In contrast, the Sungs worked hard so that their son, Hung, could complete high school in their native country. He and his parents are proud of his success during his three years of high school English instruction. He was an A student, excelling in exams on Shakespeare and Henry James. Hung will attend a two-year college, hoping eventually to earn a business degree from a university. He will take his first economics course this fall, along with a required course in basic science.

What all of the Sungs have in common is the need to read nonprose material in English. The elder Sungs will need some survival reading skills: reading bus or train schedules, classified ads, signs and labels, and instructions of all sorts. Their son will need to interpret the graphs, charts, and diagrams that accompany the prose in his college texts. For each of them, nonprose reading in English will pose new challenges. The approaches to reading introduced in Chapter One will serve the Sungs well in reading nonprose material; these same approaches will prove useful in reading many other types of texts as well.

We can use the Sung family to demonstrate some techniques of working with nonprose reading for both beginning and advanced students. Limited English proficient adults like the elder Sungs will likely attend a survival English course; such courses typically meet a couple of times each week. In addition to his other college courses, Hung will attend a daily English for academic purposes class at the local college. Both types of ESOL classes will approach the reading process in similar ways; both will introduce strategies for reading nonprose material. But, as demonstrated by the sample lessons below, students at different levels, with different purposes for reading, will encounter different kinds of texts in an ESOL reading lesson.

ACTIVATING SCHEMATA/READING INTERACTIVELY

In both sample lessons below, *students* will read material that is relevant to their communicative needs. *The teacher* will work as a facilitator, helping students to provide their own solutions and approaches to language problems. A range of *formats* will be utilized including full-class discussion and activities completed by small groups, pairs, and individuals.

Sample Lesson 1: Nonprose Reading in a Survival English Class

This evening, in the Sungs' survival English class, students have been examining the classified advertisements in newspapers. A variety of techniques is used to introduce and activate information students will need if they are to successfully read classified ads:

- The unit is introduced by a lengthy discussion of the kinds of information available in classifieds. Students discuss their experience with newspaper ads and their frustrations with the abbreviations. Eventually, the teacher focuses on employment advertisements, because many of the students are still looking for jobs. The class will examine other types of classified ads in the future whenever members of the class need to make purchases or find a place to live.
- The teacher asks the students to name the types of jobs they might look for. The responses are wide-ranging including bank teller, clerk, painter, accountant, driver, or electrician. The teacher supplies needed vocabulary and transcribes responses on the board.

- Next, the students work in groups, brainstorming the kinds of information available in employment ads, for example, whether or not experience or references are required, whether the job is full- or part-time, the number of hours worked per week, and the benefits. As groups compare their responses, the teacher, once again, works as a scribe, supplying vocabulary when necessary.
- In the same groups, students work on a vocabulary from context exercise that reinforces much of the vocabulary necessary for the concepts they have generated in their groups. Part of the exercise is reproduced below. Vocabulary items that the teacher has not anticipated can be presented in a follow-up activity in the next session.

Understanding the Help Wanted Ads

Directions: Read the following sentences and discuss with your group the meanings of unfamiliar expressions and words.

1. Mary works in a restaurant. She works 40 *hours per week.*

2. Alan wants to get a job as a mechanic, but he never finished high school. He doesn't have a *high school diploma.*

3. Tony has a *full-time* job as an electronics assembler. He works 40 hours per week.

4. Sally called on the telephone about a job downtown. The supervisor told Sally to come downtown and *apply in person.*

5. Alex called about a job and the supervisor told him to send a *resume.* The supervisor wanted to see a list of all of Alex's skills and jobs.

6. Bill saw an ad in the paper for dishwashers. Bill has never worked in a restaurant before, but he might get the job anyway, because *no experience is required.*

7. The boss told Alice to put three *references* on her job application. The boss might call these people later to make sure Alice is a good worker.

8. Doris is a secretary. She gets very good *benefits.* She has health insurance and three weeks of paid vacation time.

(Exercise adapted from Bruce McCutcheon, 1987.)

- For homework students are asked to bring to class the Sunday edition of the local newspaper, *The Evening Star.*
- When the students enter the room for the next class meeting, they find written on the board a list of jobs in which individuals have expressed interest. Students work in pairs to locate and decipher ads in their newspapers for similar jobs.
- Next, the class as a whole deciphers a few representative ads. At first, the teacher calls students' attention to particular items, but soon students are pointing out ads on their own. The teacher is careful to note that there is no standard abbreviation format. Different newspapers will use different conventions; students will need to use logic and context to guess the meanings of classified abbreviations.
- The following exercise is begun with class members volunteering oral responses; students finish the exercise in writing, working individually.

Help Wanted Ads in *The Evening Star*

Directions: Look in the help wanted ads (figure 3.1.) of *The Evening Star* newspaper. Answer the following questions:

1. Tell me about the kitchen helper job.
2. What does the mechanic for elevators need to have?
3. Is the pay for the auto mechanic good or not very good?
4. If you want to be a teacher's assistant, do you need to have experience?
5. When should you apply for the shipping clerk job?
6. Is the job for a wig stylist part-time or full-time?
7. What do you need for the janitor job?
8. Could you apply for the job as a travel agent?

- For homework, students are to find an ad in the next evening's newspaper to which they might actually apply.

Discussion of the Lesson

In the activities described above, notice how the instructor introduced and activated knowledge about the reading task at hand. Students began by discussing what they knew about classified ads and what they found confusing (i.e., abbreviations). New vocabulary was introduced so that students could begin deciphering what had once seemed indecipherable. The new vocabulary allowed students to form hypotheses about the kinds of ads they would find in the newspaper, and to discover, on their own, whether they had been correct. Armed with new information,

Figure 3.1. Help Wanted Ads

THE EVENING STAR

333
HELP WANTED

ACCT clerk. Knowledge of 10-key and typing nec., 1 yr. exp. pref. Send resume to this paper ad no. 8239.

AUTO BODY repair person, gd. mechanical skills req. Own tools nec. 343-9823 after 5.

AUTO mechanic, must have foreign car exp. and metric tools. Gd. pay, benefits, wkg. conditions. 782-2721

BAKERY counter workers. Full-or part-time. No exp. req. Will train. 751-7931

BILLING CLERK, figure aptitude nec., gd. typist pref., local ref. req. 341-1900.

BKKPR. p/t 5 yrs. exp. req. Must be bondable and have gd. refs. Call 926-9369 for appt.

CAB
DRIVERS

Must have Calif. drvs. lic., w/gd. rec. Must be over 25 yrs. old. Apply in person Mon., Tues. & Fri. only. 11th and Harrison.

CARPENTER, 6 yr. exp. req. lic. desired. Call 530-7476 evenings only.

CASHIER, must be bondable, local exp. req. 397-1942.

CLERK typist. General ofc. exp. req., knowledge of duplicating machines helpful. Call 362-9209.

COOK, p/t evenings. Apply in person. 8001 Sunset Ave.

DENTAL Asst., M/F, exp. req., X-ray lic. helpful. 531-7763.

ELECTRICIAN, f.t., lic. req., plant exp. pref. Call 380-2700.

GARDENER, exp. nec. Send resume to P. Kennedy, 272 Post St., San Francisco, CA 94109.

HOTEL DESK CLERK, 40 hr. wk. NCR 4200 exp. nec. Call for interview Mon-Fri 2-4 p.m. 474-6464

JANITORIAL, $4/hr., day wk. only. Drvers. lic. and ref. req. 244-2170.

KITCHEN helper, p.t., exp. req. Apply 5740 Lake St.

MECHANIC, elevator. Must have h.s. diploma, exp. req. 231-4383.

MEDICAL receptionist, exp. req., must be gd. at typing Write this paper, ad no. 541.

PAINTER, 3 yrs. local exp. pref. Must have H.S. diploma. Own car and equip. req. Call 876-3252 for interview.

PBX
OPERATORS

f.t. perm. to work swing shift. 1 yr. exp. req. $4.25/hr. 204-0900

PLUMBERS, service and repair exp. req., must have lic., own tools helpful. 328-2277.

RECEPTIONIST/Typist, p.t., must be accurate typist, knowledge of filing and billing helpful. Call Rose at 213-3569.

RESTAURANT help, American food exp. nec., M-F. Call 845-3009.

SALESPERSON, f.t., perm., furniture store. No exp. req. Will train. Call Mr. Wells, 477-2515.

SECRETARY, shorthand 80 wpm, typing 70 wpm. 2 yr. exp. req. Figure aptitude desired. Send resume to 3600 W. 3rd.

SERVICE STATION attendant, local ref. req. Apply M-F, 9-3, 1200 9th Ave.

SEWING machine operator, 6 mos. exp. nec. Apply 9 a.m.-4 p.m., 1444 Pine St.

SHIPPING CLERK. Drvrs. lic. pref. Must be able to lift 80 pounds. Apply 370 Market, 1:30-3 p.m.

TEACHER ASST., ref. req. exp. desired. Send resume to 3001 Harrison, San Francisco 94109.

TRAVEL AGENT, 2 yrs. exp. req., bilingual Spanish/English pref. Call 648-5887.

TRUCK
DRIVERS

Min. 5 yrs. exp. gd. driving rec. pref. Call 746-7891 from 8-5.

TYPIST, must type 70 wpm accurately. Phn. skills pref. Good sal. and benefits. Call Pam for appt., 568-6277, ext. 48, 9 a.m.-5 p.m., Mon.-Fri.

WAITER/WAITRESS, local exp. req. Apply in person, 5332 East 10th St.

WIG stylist. Perm., f.t. 421-9824.

WINDOW cleaner, wk. all shifts. No exp. req. Will train. 262-9013.

X-RAY
TECHNICIAN

p.t., in hospital, lic. req., 1 yr. exp. pref. Send resume to Mills Hospital, 100 19th Ave.

Exercise adapted from *Using the Help Wanted Ads* by B. McCutcheon, unpublished manuscript, University of Washington, Seattle; *Evening Star* ads from *English That Works* (p. 164) by K. L. Savage, M. How, and E. L. Yueng, 1982, Glenview, Ill.: Scott, Foresman.

and a full discussion of their preexisting background knowledge, students were able to successfully read the want ads to determine the qualifications and application procedures for a series of real jobs. Reading interactively, they were able to determine which ads were appropriate for them. *Note that in the context of immigrant education it is especially important to begin with students' expectations and desires if one is to avoid channeling students into entry-level dead-end jobs.*

Students moved toward increasing independence in reading as they worked to meet real communicative goals. In subsequent lessons students will combine their ability to read want ads with other language skill work as they practice job interviews and filling out applications.

Notice that the activities focused on both bottom-up and top-down processing. Attention was drawn to abbreviations and other aspects of the text to facilitate bottom-up (data-driven) processing. Students used knowledge of employment ads and jobs for top-down (conceptually driven) information processing.

Sample Lesson 2: Nonprose Reading in an English for Academic Purposes Class

At an advanced level, similar techniques can be used. In his ESOL class, Hung, an economics major, has been reading college-level social science passages containing nonprose material. As in the survival English course, the academic English instructor can provide and access appropriate background information and help students use reading material to meet their own needs:

- In Hung's class, students have been examining the role of nonprose evidence (charts, graphs, diagrams, etc.) in academic argumentation. Students have decided to research the so-called population explosion.
- The instructor provides students with an article on the topic from a college-level textbook for native speakers. An initial discussion helps students develop a set of expectations for an article on the burgeoning world population. Part of the class discussion centers on the type of nonprose evidence one might expect to accompany an article on this topic.
- Students read quickly to determine the author's approach and to see if their expectations concerning nonprose evidence are confirmed.
- Students then reread, carefully, for a more detailed and critical understanding of the evidence presented. Careful reading will allow students to evaluate the evidence and argumentation with respect to their previous knowledge and personal beliefs.

- Students may decide to read a series of articles on the same topic, building necessary background knowledge in order to read increasingly complex arguments and data. Such substantial work in a content area will aid in developing a core vocabulary on the subject.
- Reading and research projects can be combined with writing instruction. For the next class hour, students write a critical review comparing the articles they have read on this topic.

Discussion of the Lesson

Notice that the instructor was able to present material relevant to students' academic interests. Relevance established, a prereading discussion presented and accessed knowledge about the topic at hand. As students read more on the topic, they will approach successive texts with an increasing store of knowledge and more detailed and sophisticated expectations. This iterative approach to texts—hypothesis formation, initial reading, rereading, and evaluating—will prove generalizable to students' independent academic pursuits.

For all the Sungs, their formal English studies will be short-lived. In their coursework they will need to acquire approaches to texts that will serve them well when they are reading entirely on their own. The types of activities outlined in this chapter are designed to provide students with techniques for working with texts outside the ESOL class.

Below are some additional examples of instructional formats; most are taken from commercially available textbooks. Some of these formats are easily adaptable for teacher-developed materials. Others are more easily located in existing textbooks. Chapter Seven explores issues of materials development.

READING NONPROSE TEXTS FOR GENERAL UNDERSTANDING

There are many instances when readers need only obtain a general sense of a text. Examples include skimming a menu to see if one can afford to eat in a particular restaurant, or quickly examining a passage to see if it merits careful reading. Students at every proficiency level can benefit from practice in skimming both prose and nonprose material.

In Mr. and Mrs. Sung's survival English class, students practice interpreting the function of various nonprose material so that they will be able to quickly and appropriately respond to signs, instructions, and the like. Their son learns to recognize the function of nonprose academic material. Here are some examples of both types of activities. Note that either format below can be used at any proficiency level.

Nonprose Skimming: Multiple Choice/Matching

Directions: Choose the best answer. Which of these notices (figure 3.2) would you see

_____ **a.** in a house?
_____ **b.** in a public building?
_____ **c.** in a railway station?
_____ **d.** in a zoo?
_____ **e.** in a museum?

Figure 3.2. Everyday Notices

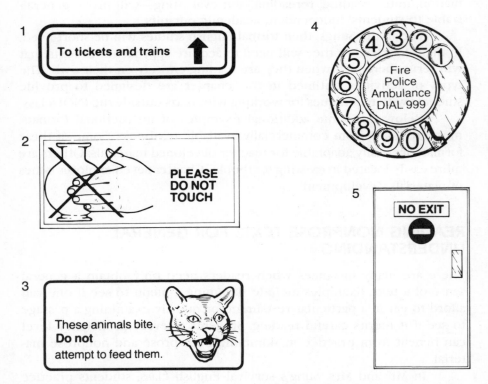

1 To tickets and trains

2 PLEASE DO NOT TOUCH

3 These animals bite. **Do not** attempt to feed them.

4 5 4 3 2 1 / 6 7 8 9 0 Fire Police Ambulance DIAL 999

5 NO EXIT

Adapted from *Reading and Thinking in English: Exploring Functions* (pp. 2–3), Associate Editor H.G. Widdowson, 1979, Oxford: Oxford University Press.

Figure 3.3. The March of Time

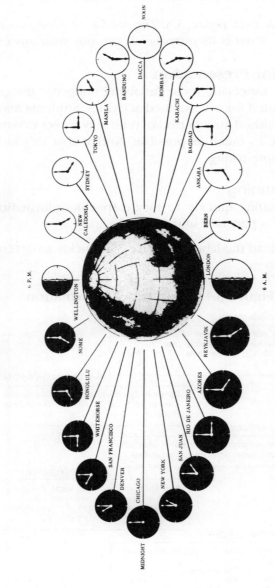

From *Breaking the Reading Barrier* (p. 68) by D. W. Gilbert, 1959, Englewood Cliffs, N.J.: Prentice Hall.

27

Nonprose Skimming: Open-ended

A series of tasks can be presented like the following:

Directions: Look over figure 3.3, *The March of Time*, on p. 27. Study its general plan. What is its purpose? Write out your answer.

Suggestions for Presentation

Skimming tasks, especially those involving nonprose material, are particularly well suited for use as timed activities. Students may work until the last one is finished, or a period of time may be set in which students are to complete as much as possible. Notice that this task combines skimming and note-taking.

Nonprose Scanning

Scanning is reading quickly to locate specific information. The first example below is part of a unit on food.

1. Directions: Read the labels in figure 3.4 quickly to determine which have food additives.

Figure 3.4. Food Label Information

CHICKEN SOUP

Chicken stock, tomatoes, rice, chicken, water, celery, salt, starch, sugar, peppers, yeast, natural flavoring, artificial color.
Calories per 5 oz	70	Carbohydrate	10 g
Protein	2 g	Fat	2 g

INSTANT MASHED POTATOES

Dehydrated potatoes, salt, calcium disodium.
Calories per ⅓ cup	60	Carbohydrate	14 g
Protein	2 g	Fat	0 g

CHOPPED BEEF FROZEN DINNER

Water, flour, cooked beef, shortening, carrots, starch, peas, salt, vegetable protein, potatoes, sugar, artificial color, spices, BHA.

FROZEN FISH STICKS

Fish fillets, enriched flour, sugar, nonfat dry milk, starch, salt, water, soybean oil, baking powder, eggs.
Calories per 4 sticks	230	Carbohydrate	24 g
Protein	10 g	Fat	10 g

SALTINE CRACKERS

Enriched wheat flour (vitamins added), vegetable shortening, salt, calcium propitionate, yeast.
Calories per 10 crackers	120	Carbohydrate	20 g
		Fat	4 g
Protein	3 g		

From *Read Right! Developing Survival Reading Skills* (p. 4) by A. U. Chamot, 1982, New York: Minerva.

The second example would accompany a technical article.

2. Directions: Using the information in figure 3.5, write T (true) or F (false) in the parentheses beside the statements that follow.

Figure 3.5. Temperature Graph

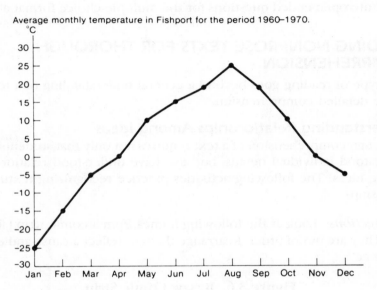

Average monthly temperature in Fishport for the period 1960–1970.

T (true) or F (false)?

1. The average January temperature in Fishport for the period 1960–1970 was 25°C.   1. ( )
2. For the period 1960–1970, the average July temperature in Fishport was the same as the temperature in September.   2. ( )
3. Like those in March, December temperatures averaged −5°C.   3. ( )
4. In Fishport, January, February, and March were all colder than December during the decade for which we have data.   4. ( )
5. On average, neither July nor September was as hot as August.   5. ( )

From *Reading English for Academic Study* (p. 10) by M. H. Long, W. Allen, A. Cyr, C. Pomeroy, E. Ricard, N. Spada, and P. Vogel, 1980, Rowley, Mass.: Newbury House.

Suggestions for Presentation

Note that graphs and tables are generally accompanied by prose text. Though it can be useful to introduce students to nonprose reading in isolation, later activities should provide practice in synthesizing related prose and nonprose material. As with skimming, scanning activities can profitably be timed. Note that a somewhat more authentic format would substitute open-ended questions for the multiple-choice format above.

READING NONPROSE TEXTS FOR THOROUGH COMPREHENSION

This type of reading goes beyond a general understanding of a text to assure detailed comprehension.

Understanding Relationships Among Ideas

Thorough comprehension of a text requires not only that students have understood individual details, but also have understood relationships among ideas. The following activities practice recognizing textual relationships.

1. *Directions:* Look at the following frames from a comic strip (figure 3.6). They are out of order. Rearrange them to reflect a cause and effect sequence.

Figure 3.6. Jigsaw Comic Strip

From *Reading by Doing: An Introduction to Effective Reading* (p. 60) by J. S. Simmons, B. C. Palmer, and A. Berger, 1983, Skokie, Ill.: National Textbook Company.

This type of activity, in which students rearrange text in order to (re)create a logical sequence, is often called **jigsaw reading.**

The following activity requires that students demonstrate their understanding of the relations of components in a solar collector by labeling parts of a diagram. In order to complete this task, students need to be able to synthesize information from the prose passage and the partially labeled diagram.

2. *Directions:* Read the following paragraph. It describes a solar collector (figure 3.7). When you finish the paragraph, label the parts of the diagram on page 32.

SOLAR COLLECTORS

One type of solar collector is not very expensive. It is put on the roof of a building. It is usually put on the sunny side of the roof. The sun is most direct on this side, and the unit will collect more heat from the sun. The unit has a flat or level surface. The surface is black because black collects more heat from the sun. Inside, there are **pipes** with water. The **top** is a piece of glass. The sun shines through the glass and air inside. It heats the water that is also inside. A **pump**, a machine to move the water, starts when water is warm enough. Then hot water goes into a storage **tank**. This tank stores or keeps the hot water. Then there is hot water to use for washing clothes or taking baths and showers.

(*continued*)

Figure 3.7. Solar Collector

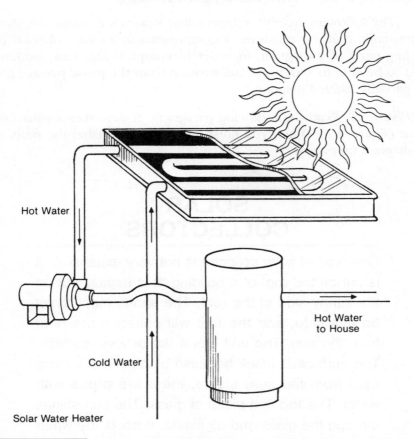

Hot Water

Hot Water
to House

Cold Water

Solar Water Heater

From *Momentum: Developing Reading Skills* (pp. 70–71) by B. L. Sosna and H. T. Abdulaziz, 1985, New York: Holt, Rinehart and Winston.

Suggestions for Presentation

This type of activity can be organized either for pair or group work. In the case of jigsaw reading, students work together to solve the puzzle; each student is provided a different piece of the text. When working with diagrams (such as in the solar collector passage above), students can work together, moving between prose and nonprose material, to complete the diagram. In this instance, listening and reading activities can be combined: one student reads the prose to others who must complete the diagram.

CRITICAL READING OF NONPROSE TEXTS

Critical reading requires going beyond literal understanding in order to draw inferences and evaluate a text. Readers determine, for example, how an idea fits into their own system of beliefs. Reading critically, the questions one asks vary depending on the text and one's purpose for reading.

Drawing Inferences

Following is an activity that requires drawing inferences about the functions and meanings of a nonprose text.

1. *Directions:* Read the following notice (figure 3.8).

Figure 3.8. Public Notice

FISH FOR FUN!
DO NOT FISH FOR FOOD!

FISHERMEN!
FOR THE PROTECTION
OF YOUR HEALTH,
FISH FROM THESE WATERS
SHOULD NOT BE EATEN
BECAUSE OF MERCURY
CONTAMINATION.
Department of Land and Forests

Now answer these questions:

1. Is the function of the notice to give information, to warn or to give an order?
2. Where would people see the notice?
3. Can people fish where they see the notice?
4. What must they not do?
5. What warning is given by the picture?
6. What will happen if people do not follow the warning?

Adapted from *Reading and Thinking in English: Exploring Functions* (p. 5), Associate Editor H. G. Widdowson, 1979, Oxford: Oxford University Press.

The following activity would be useful in preparing ESOL students to read engineering material. Students will need to apply preexisting knowledge and to draw inferences based on the diagrams, in order to complete the exercise reproduced in figure 3.9.

2. *Directions:* Complete the following sentences to describe the relations shown in the diagrams. Use the verbs given in the list.

Figure 3.9. Engineering Diagrams

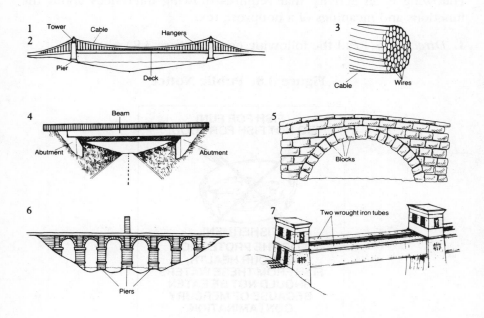

run through
be connected to
be made up of
interlock
be supported by
consist of
be joined together by
rest on

1. The deck......a cable by hangers.

2. Each tower......a pier.

3. Each cable......thousands of parallel wires.

4. The beam......abutments at each end.

5. In an arch bridge the blocks......to form a semicircle.

6. Continuous bridges......two or more beam bridges, which......piers.

7. One type of railway bridge has two wrought iron tubes. A railway line......each tube.

From *Reading and Thinking in English: Exploring Functions* (p. 42), Associate Editor H. G. Widdowson, 1979, Oxford: Oxford University Press.

Evaluating Texts in Terms of One's System of Beliefs

Students may be given opportunities to render information relevant to their cultural context.

The following example from a survival English class would be preceded by a lesson on nutrition.

1. *Directions:* Now that you have read some suggestions for packing bag lunches, plan some lunches yourself. Using the foods listed in figure 3.10 (you may add other foods to it), describe a healthful and delicious packed lunch for each of the three people described on the next page.

Figure 3.10. Nutritious Lunch Planner

PROTEIN (choose 1)		VEGETABLE (choose 1,2 If no fruit)	FRUIT (choose 1,2 If no vegetable)	BEVERAGE (choose 1)	DESSERT (optional)
Sandwich	**Non-sandwich***				
Chopped egg	Chicken wings or drumstick	Celery	Melon wedge or balls	Milk (preferred) (or yogurt)	Sunflower seeds and raisins
Sardine, Salmon or tuna salad with lettuce	Cheese sticks rolled in bologna	Carrots	Plum	Orange juice	Cookies
Swiss cheese with lettuce	Cottage cheese with pineapple	Green pepper strips	Fruit salad	Tomato juice	Fruit flavored yogurt
White fish with cat- sup & parsley	Stew	Fresh tomato (sections or cherry)	Apple	Grapefruit juice	Peanut butter granola balls
Peanut butter and banana	Soup	Cucumber	Orange wedges	Apricot nectar	
Baked bean on wheat bread	Chili	Cauliflower with mayonnaise dip	Pineapple cubes (fresh or canned)	Apple juice or cider	Fresh fruit
	Peanut butter in celery sticks	Coleslaw	Banana	Pineapple juice	Fruit bars
Cottage cheese & raisin on Boston brown bread	Cubes of ham and cheese	Grated carrot- raisin-nut salad	Berries		Dried fruit
			Cherries		Nuts
Scrambled egg	Tuna fish salad	Three bean salad	Peach		Yogurt with fruit
Sliced turkey & lettuce on biscuit	Green pepper or apple stuffed with cottage cheese mixed with veg- etable or raisins and nuts	Watercress	Grapes		Popcorn sprinkled with cheese
Cheddar cheese & bean sprouts		Kohlrabi			
Chopped chicken liver on rye		Peeled broccoli stems			
meat loaf		Zucchini strips			
Roast beef		Fresh peas			
		Avocado slices			

*If you're not eating a sandwich, include some other starch like potato or rice salad, a muffin or roll.

Reprinted with permission from *Bag It* by Giant Food, Inc., 1976. All rights reserved.

From *Reading Right: Developing Survival Reading Skills* (p. 15) by A. U. Chamot, 1982, New York: Minerva.

Bag lunch for an eight-year-old child at school	Bag lunch for an overweight adult	Bag lunch for a busy person who works in an office
_____	_____	_____
_____	_____	_____
_____	_____	_____
_____	_____	_____
_____		

Comic strips provide useful practice in drawing cultural inferences and evaluating human behavior in terms of students' own systems of beliefs.

2. *Directions:* The cartoon reproduced in figure 3.11 represents a cartoonist's view of modern relationships and family life. Try to answer the following questions:

1. In what ways is the portrayal familiar to you?
2. In what ways does it seem strange?
3. Would this cartoon be considered funny in your country/community?
4. Do you find it funny?

Figure 3.11. "Love Handles"

Suggestions for Presentation

Although inferencing is a private enterprise, it easily accommodates group work. Students can read on their own, drawing inferences and developing individual interpretations of texts. Inferences are then compared in groups. Predictably, debates will develop, necessitating that students return to the text to demonstrate the **comprehending process.**

SPECIAL FEATURES OF NONPROSE TEXTS

Nonprose material can prove an important component of a reading curriculum. For some students, this kind of reading will be new. In the case of the Sungs, for example, the parents may be confronting the necessity of using road maps or bus schedules for the first time. Their son's experience reading literature has not prepared him for the graphs and tables he will encounter. Activities that introduce nonprose materials will provide the Sungs with important reading skills.

On the other hand, focusing on familiar nonprose material may furnish an opportunity to capitalize on previous knowledge. Although the elder Sungs may not believe that they can read English, they will be surprised at the number of street signs and product labels they quickly recognize. Their teacher can take advantage of this preexisting knowledge to demonstrate the utility of rapid reading; she can introduce new material and concepts by building lessons around schemata that students already possess.

Nonprose material affords opportunities for productive practice in both top-down and bottom-up processing. Students rely on prior knowledge as they learn to interpret familiar types of nonprose material. The rate-building and rapid recognition activities invited by nonprose material help build the automaticity recommended by current research.

Perhaps the most important feature of nonprose material is that it often accompanies prose, for example, the statistical tables that appear in technical articles. By calling students' attention to nonprose material, we can demonstrate the interaction between prose and nonprose portions of texts. Just as nonprose material is integrated into many prose texts, it should be integrated into the ESOL reading class.

SUMMARY

At all proficiency levels, students can use the following types of materials to practice interpreting nonprose material. Tasks should entail problem solving, utilizing both previous knowledge and information found in texts.

Maps from public transportation, street maps, and road maps with mileage tables can be used to practice receiving and giving directions, and determining the most efficient route.

Graphs and tables often accompany technical prose. Inefficient readers rely on one aspect of the text at the expense of the other. Reading tasks can be developed that require students to work back and forth, discovering how information in the graphs and tables supplements and explicates the prose.

Charts and tables may also accompany nontechnical material; for example, the mileage charts and tables that appear with road maps. Reading this material can seem a formidable task for students accustomed to receiving this information orally. Nonprose activities can demonstrate that similar skills are used to interpret most written texts.

Diagrams may accompany prose and provide important information and clues for comprehension. Diagrams may also be developed by students to help them understand or remember information in texts. (This technique is discussed in Chapter Four.) Students can be provided with practice in developing, completing, and comprehending diagrams.

Comic strips can be used to practice recognizing relationships among ideas in texts. Additionally, comic strips rely on cultural presuppositions that allow students to practice their critical reading skills.

·ACTIVITIES·

1. Develop a set of scanning questions based on the table reproduced below.

Cost of Living of United Nations Personnel in Selected Cities[1]
(New York City, December 1990 = 100)

City	Index	City	Index
Abu Dhabi	92[2]	Islamabad	80
Addis Ababa	94[2]	Jakarta	82
Algiers	96[2]	Kabul	119
Amman	89	Kathmandu	84
Ankara	80	Kingston	71
Athens	92	Kinshasa	87[2]
Baghdad	132[2]	La Paz	62
Bangkok	79	Lagos	89[2]
Beirut	78	Lima	95
Belgrade	108	London	120
Bogota	83	Madrid	123
Bonn	125	Managua	94
Brazzaville	111[2]	Manila	75
Brussels	103	Mexico City	80
Budapest	54	Montevideo	85
Buenos Aires	90	Montreal	91
Cairo	90	Nairobi	85
Caracas	87	Nassau	112
Colombo	78	New Delhi	83
Copenhagen	116	Panama City	80
Dhaka	81	Paris	117
Dakar	112	Port-au-Prince	89
Dar es Salaam	86[2]	Quito	73
Geneva	138	Rabat	87
Guatemala City	82	Rome	115
The Hague	107	Roseau	95
Helsinki	131	San Salvador	70

39

(*continued*)

Cost of Living of United Nations Personnel in Selected Cities[1] (*continued*)

(New York City, December 1990 = 100)

City	Index	City	Index
Santiago	68	Tunis	81
Seoul	112	Valetta	81
Sofia	60	Vienna	117
Sydney	88	Warsaw	45
Tokyo	137	Washington, DC	92
Tripoli	119[2]	Yangon	102

[1]Based on Index of Retail Prices, 1990.
[2]Government or subsidized housing, which is normally lower in cost.
Source: United Nations, *Monthly Bulletin of Statistics,* March 1991.

Adapted from *The 1992 Information Please Almanac* (p. 140), 1992,
Boston: Houghton Mifflin.

2. Prepare a unit on household emergencies.
   a. Develop a series of questions/activities which activate and provide background information for household emergencies.
   b. Develop case studies like the example provided which utilize
   the emergency chart in figure 3.12.

   A family goes on a picnic in the country. There are a lot of wild
   mushrooms growing near them which look exactly like the ones they
   buy in the supermarket. They pick some and decide to eat them that
   evening. The 13-year-old daughter is the only member of the family
   who hates mushrooms, so she eats a hamburger instead. Some of the
   mushrooms were poisonous. What should the daughter do?

3. Find an English language map of your city or campus or use the one
reproduced in figure 3.13 on page 42. Develop a set of activities that
   a. introduces necessary vocabulary
   b. introduces map reading
   c. requires communicative interaction among students to identify
   routes and locations.

4. Find a comic strip that would be appropriate for practicing cultural
inferencing. Develop several discussion questions to accompany the
comics. Could you scramble the comic strip to practice recognizing
relationships among ideas?

5. Find an example of a textbook article that combines prose and
nonprose material. Develop a set of true/false questions that requires
students to use information from both the prose and nonprose text.

6. Develop a (set of) task(s) that entails synthesizing prose and nonprose material.

Figure 3.12. Accidental Poisoning Responses

Listed here are more than 35 substances that often are the cause of accidental poisoning. After each one is a letter of the alphabet, keyed to the chart below the list.

In any poisoning emergency, try to identify the offending substance. (For example, "Iodine.") Then check the list for it, and note what the key letter is for it. (For example, the key letter for iodine would be "C"). Look under that letter in the section below, and you'll quickly see what to do for that particular kind of poisoning.

Acids – **I**	(e.g., chlorine) – **D**	Polishes: Floor – **J**
Alcohol, rubbing – **B**	Flypaper – **B**	Shoe – **J**
Alcohol, denatured – **F**	Gasoline – **J**	Removers: For varnish,
Alcohol, wood – **F**	Headache remedies – **B**	paint & nail polish,
Ammonia water – **G**	Insecticides – **H**	containing acetone – **A**
Aspirin – **B**	Iodine – **C**	For nail polish cont. amyl
Automobile exhaust	Kerosene – **J**	acetate – **N**
gases – **M**	Laundry bleach – **D**	Roach and Rat poisons:
Camphor – **A**	Lead – **H**	Arsenic – **B**
Carbon Tetrachloride	Lye – **G**	Fluorides – **O**
(if swallowed – **K**)	Mothballs – **A**	Phosphorus – **E**
(if inhaled – **C**)	Mushrooms – **H**	Thallium compounds – **A**
Cleaning fluids – **K**	Naphtha – **J**	Sedatives – **K**
Detergent powders – **G**	Paint (cont. lead) – **H**	Sleeping pills – **K**
DDT insecticide – **H**	Paint thinner – **H**	Turpentine – **H**
Disinfectants	Plants (poisonous) – **L**	Waxes, floor – **J**

A GET THE PATIENT TO VOMIT with:
a) One tablespoon of mustard in a glass of warm water
b) One tablespoon of salt, ditto
c) Insert spoon handle or finger in throat; press down back of tongue
Place victim face down, with head lower than hips.
Give plenty of strong tea or coffee.
Don't give alcohol in any form.

B Induce vomiting, as in "A." Then give a mixture of the following:
2 tablespoons powdered charcoal (or use powdered burnt toast)
1 tablespoon milk of magnesia
4 tablespoons very strong tea
Follow with 2 cups strong coffee or tea.

C Get patient to swallow large quantities of starchy substances (such as flour or bread or cracker crumbs) with water. Induce vomiting, as in "A." Repeat until blue color has disappeared from vomit.

D Get patient to vomit, as in "A." Get patient to swallow liberal amounts of milk and egg white, to help dilute poison in stomach. Give patient two cups of strong tea or coffee, mixed with egg whites.

E Induce vomiting as in "A." Administer epsom salt solution (1 tablespoon salt in a glass of warm water), and one-half cup of mineral oil (not animal fat or vegetable oil).

F Get patient to vomit, as in "A." Administer baking soda solution (1 tablespoon soda in two glasses water).
Repeat process until alcohol odor is no longer detectable.

G DO NOT INDUCE VOMITING Give victim a mixture of vinegar and water, or liberal quantities of citrus fruit juices. Follow with glasses of milk.
If lye has been swallowed, rush patient to hospital.

H Get patient to vomit, as in "A." Give epsom salt solution (two tablespoons salts in one pint of water. One pint = 2 glasses.) Have patient drink two cups strong tea or coffee.

I DON'T INDUCE VOMITING. Instead, give milk of magnesia, milk mixed with a liberal amount of water, or beaten egg whites.

J DON'T INDUCE VOMITING Have patient drink 4 ounces of mineral oil, plus several cups of coffee or tea.

K Get patient to vomit, as in "A." Have patient drink two cups of strong tea or coffee. Give patient artificial respiration if required.

L Get patient to vomit, as in "A." Identify the plant which has been eaten and call your physician for instructions.

M Move patient away from source of fumes and into uncontaminated air. Keep patient warm and encourage resting. If required, provide artificial respiration.

N Give lots of strong coffee or tea. Immediately ask doctor for advice on treatment.

O Induce vomiting, as in "A." Have patient drink liberal amounts of milk.

HANG CHART IN CONVENIENT LOCATION OR TAPE IT TO BACK OF MEDICINE CABINET DOOR.

Adapted from *Read Right! Developing Survival Reading Skills* (p. 87) by A. U. Chamot, 1982, New York: Minerva.

Figure 3.13. Mexico City Map

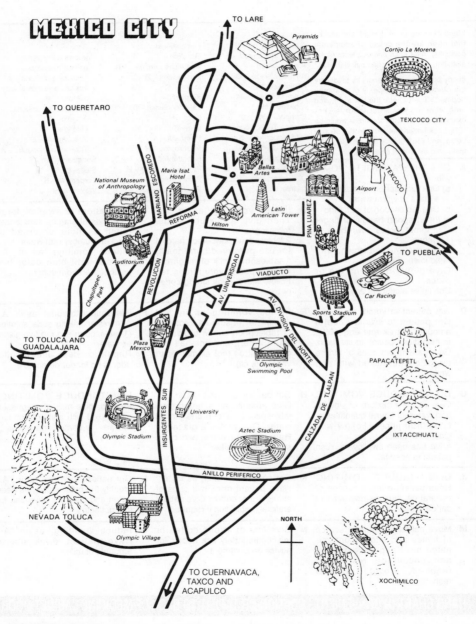

From *Start Reading* (p. 45), 1983, New York: Pergamon.

·CHAPTER FOUR·
EXPOSITORY PROSE

Expository prose dominates most second language reading curricula. Students learn to understand and interpret written arguments. This type of reading is central for students who will use English for academic purposes (EAP).

Our sample lessons in this chapter will focus on an EAP classroom. We find these instructional settings throughout the world: in English-speaking countries; in locations where English is used as a mode of instruction throughout the curriculum, particularly in universities; and in countries where English is encountered only in English language classes.

Reading components of EAP classes provide students with opportunities to read expository prose typical of their disciplines. There is explicit attention to the discourse conventions and grammatical features typical of academic writing in general and of specific fields of study.

SAMPLE LESSON

As an example, we will look at activities in an EAP class for students of the social sciences. In many ways, this context is not very different from the other settings we have observed. In particular, the teacher tries to focus on reading tasks that are appropriate to the students' needs and interests. The instructor avoids unmotivated assignments, concentrating instead on readings from students' fields of study. Often the students are asked to bring to class textbooks that they will be studying in other courses.

Students discuss a text in advance to develop a context in which to read and to develop expectations about what they will find. Often students will preview a text, noting its overall organization and the clues to content and point of view available from an initial rapid overview. Students generally read with a particular goal in mind that will help determine the strategies with which to approach a text.

Prereading Activities

Our class of social science students has been discussing academic approaches to studying the family. They are about to begin looking at their first scholarly article, in this case from the United States. The following activities are designed to take place before the students read the entire article.

Class discussion anticipating content:*

1. What do you already know about the family in the United States? What "facts" do you know; what opinions do you hold?
2. What events may have affected the development of the U.S. family?
3. On the basis of your knowledge, what do you think the article will say about the development of the family in the U.S.?

Students discover that they have conflicting and not always favorable knowledge and assumptions about U.S. families. In groups, students discuss their reactions to the topic and develop hypotheses about the data they will encounter in the article. Students then **preview** the text, using textual clues to develop an overall sense of the content.

Previewing

Students complete the following activities in pairs, working back and forth between the text and paired discussion:*

1. Read the title of the article. Look to see if an author is mentioned and whether the author(s)' credentials are stated. Does this provide you with any information concerning the author(s)' point of view about the material presented?
2. Read the first few paragraphs. Then note any headings and visually emphasized terms in the rest of the article. Decide what you think are the general themes of the article.
3. Read the first sentence of several paragraphs in the article. Then read the last paragraph. What seems to be the main goal or point

*Adapted from *Contemporary Perspectives: An Advanced Reader/Rhetoric in English* (p. 5) by R. L. Saitz, M. Dezell, and F. B. Stieglitz, 1984, Boston: Little, Brown.

of view of the article? How does the author organize the information to achieve this?

Students then read the entire article for information concerning particular issues they have been researching, for example:

- the changing nature of the U.S. family (including statistical documentation)
- factors leading to changing family demographics
- attitudes towards these changes.

Predicting Content

On the second day of reading about the family, students turn their attention to another social science article on the U.S. family, beginning with prereading and previewing activities. In this instance, however, a focused reading activity intervenes in the reading process. Students are asked to stop reading at several points in order to focus attention on the process of prediction. Students work in groups, forming a context in which to consciously explore the bases for their expectations. Often expectations will rest on students' knowledge of discourse conventions typical of their fields of study. Later in this chapter we will examine in detail activities that focus on these discourse patterns. Figure 4.1 is an activity that begins to make students conscious of the ways in which they encounter written arguments.

Figure 4.1. The Changing Family

Below is part of an article about the family [*LSA* 10(3)(Spring 1987)]. Read the article, stopping to respond to the questions that appear at several points throughout. Remember, you cannot always predict precisely what an author will do, but you can use knowledge of the text and your general knowledge to make good guesses. Work with your classmates on these items, defending your predictions with parts of the text. Do not worry about unfamiliar vocabulary.

The Changing Family by Maris Vinovskis

1. Based on the title, what aspect of the family do you think this article will be about? List several possibilities.

_____

_____

 (*continued*)

Now read the opening paragraph to see what the focus of the article will be.

There is widespread fear among policymakers and the public today that the family is falling apart. Much of that worry stems from a basic misunderstanding of the nature of the family in the past and lack of appreciation for its strength in response to broad social and economic changes. The general view of the family is that it has been a stable and relatively unchanging institution through history and is only now undergoing changes; in fact, change has always been characteristic of it.

The Family and Household in the Past

2. This article seems to be about the changing nature of the family throughout history. Is this what you expected?

3. The introduction is not very specific, so you can only guess what changing aspects of the family will be mentioned in the next section. Using information from the introduction and your general knowledge, check (✓) those topics from the list below that you think will be mentioned:

_____ a. family size   _____ f.   the family throughout the world
_____ b. relations within the family   _____ g. the economic role of the family
_____ c. the definition of a family   _____ h. sex differences in family roles
_____ d. the role of family in society   _____ i.   the role of children
_____ e. different family customs   _____ j.   sexual relations

Now read the next section, noting which of your predictions is confirmed.

In the last twenty years, historians have been re-examining the nature of the family and have concluded that we must revise our notions of the family as an institution, as well as our assumptions about how children were perceived and treated in past centuries. A survey of diverse studies of the family in the West, particularly in seventeenth-, eighteenth-, and nineteenth-century England and America shows something of the changing role of the family in society and the evolution of our ideas of parenting and child development. (Although many definitions of *family* are available, in this article I will use it to refer to kin living under one roof.)

4. Which aspects of the family listed above were mentioned in this section?

_____

_____

5. Which other ones do you predict will be mentioned further on in the article?

_____

6. What aspects of the text and your general knowledge help you to create this prediction?

_____

_____

7. Below is the topic sentence of the next paragraph. What kind of supporting data do you
   expect to find in the rest of the paragraph? How do you think the paragraph will continue?

> Although we have tended to believe that in the past children grew up in "extended
> households" including grandparents, parents, and children, recent historical research has
> cast considerable doubt on the idea that as countries became increasingly urban and
> industrial, the Western family evolved from extended to nuclear (i.e., parents and
> children only).

The rest of the paragraph is reprinted below. Read on to see if your expectations are confirmed.

> Historians have found evidence that households in pre-industrial Western Europe were
> already nuclear and could not have been greatly transformed by economic changes.
> Rather than finding definite declines in household size, we find surprisingly small
> variations, which turn out to be a result of the presence or absence of servants, boarders,
> and lodgers, rather than relatives. In revising our nostalgic picture of children growing up
> in large families, Peter Laslett, one of the foremost analysts of the pre-industrial family,
> contends that most households in the past were actually quite small (mean household size
> was about 4.75). Of course, patterns may have varied somewhat from one area to another,
> but it seems unlikely that in the past few centuries many families in England or America
> had grandparents living with them.

8. Were your predictions confirmed?

9. Look again at the list of topics you saw in Question 3. Now *skim* the rest of the article;
   check (✓) the topics that the author actually discusses.

____ a. family size		____ f.	the family throughout the world
____ b. relations within the family		____ g.	the economic role of the family
____ c. the definition of a family		____ h.	sex differences in family roles
____ d. the role of family in society		____ i.	the role of children
____ e. different family customs		____ j.	sexual relations

Activity from *Reader's Choice* (2nd ed., pp. 236–238) by E. M. Baudoin, E. S. Bober,
M. A. Clarke, B. K. Dobson, and S. Silberstein, 1988, Ann Arbor, Mich.: University of
Michigan Press. Reading passage from "The Changing Family" by Maris Vinovskis, 1987,
LSA, 10 (3), Ann Arbor: The University of Michigan.

The final section of this activity facilitates practice in reading
extended prose quickly in order to ascertain whether it merits careful
study. Students in academic programs, in particular, need practice in
reading and synthesizing a great deal of written material.

Synthesizing Information

Students are now ready to read on their own. With their research questions in mind, students in our sample class distribute reading tasks among themselves. Each reads and synthesizes relevant portions of several articles brought to class by both students and teacher. As a group, they then compare and contrast the information they have accumulated concerning the changing U.S. family.

Critical Reading

Finally, students evaluate the information contained in the social science passages they have been reading. Some students feel that the information was presented too uncritically. Some find changes in the U.S. family deeply disturbing and wonder why even social science textbooks don't fully address what students see as the dangers of some demographic shifts. Others feel that the articles deal with popular perceptions too often for an academic context. Students debate the functions of texts, then move on to evaluate the actual findings and conclusions drawn. (The function of text is the province of Chapter Five.)

DISCUSSION OF THE LESSON

As was the case in the instructional settings we observed in Chapter Three, these advanced EAP students benefited from developing a context for reading.

It is important to remember that prereading and previewing activities are appropriate at all proficiency levels. For example, the beginning reading textbook *No Hot Water Tonight* asks students to consider the following questions before they read about a widow in an urban setting:*

1. Are you married or single?
2. Where are you from?
3. Where are you living?
4. Where's your apartment? (your room? your house?)

Teachers might add additional questions such as the following if appropriate for their students:

5. Do old women ever live alone in your country/community?
6. Is/was your grandmother happy?

---

*From *No Hot Water Tonight* (p. 1) by J. Bodman and M. Lanzano, 1975, New York: Collier Macmillian International.

In the context of prereading activities, it is helpful that beginning-level textbooks generally provide a great many visual clues that reward previewing.

Returning to our sample lesson, prereading and predicting activities were followed by those requiring synthesizing and evaluating texts. These tasks draw on readers' prior knowledge of those discourse conventions and grammatical features that are typical of texts in their disciplines or of written English in general. Listed below are some formats designed to develop students' familiarity with these conventions of English expository prose.

Readers may want to skim the remainder of this chapter, noting particularly those elements of expository prose fundamental to the kinds of reading their students will encounter. It is not necessary to render our students expert in discourse analysis and its metalanguage. Some of the descriptions of rhetorical patterns and genre conventions appearing later in this chapter will prove more directly useful to teachers than to lower level students. Such knowledge, however, often enables the instructor to illuminate student comprehension problems. Moreover, explicit instruction in discourse conventions can prove invaluable if these elements are fundamental to student texts.

STRUCTURING A TEXT: GENERALIZATIONS WITH SUPPORTING INFORMATION

Students can learn to recognize the structure of an argument by distinguishing between general claims and the data used to support those claims. Not every paragraph has a topic sentence, nor does every text contain a thesis statement. But expository prose tends to rely on general claims supported by details and examples. Recognizing how these are used can lead to a better understanding of an overall argument and to a more effective critique of that argument. (Critical reading will be the focus of Chapter Five.)

Semantic Maps

One technique that allows students to demonstrate their understanding of the relationships among ideas within a text is the drawing of **semantic maps.** Designed to overcome the constraints of the outline format, semantic mapping allows students the freedom to visually present a hierarchy of ideas in a diagram format that is uniquely theirs.

Figure 4.2. Semantic Maps

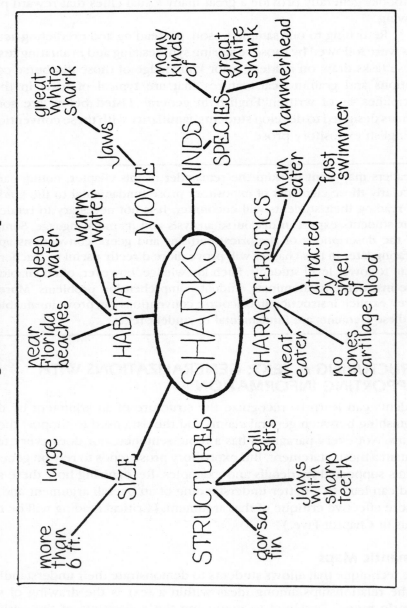

Prereading Semantic Map

ENEMIES — dolphins, whales, porpoises, man

MOVIE — Jaws

SPECIES — great white shark, 200 species, whale shark, dogfish shark, hammerhead, kinds

CHARACTERISTICS — slender streamlined shape, fast swimmer 35 knots, ventral mouth, no bones cartilaginous fish skeleton of cartilage, excellent sense of smell, attracted by smell of blood, teeth on tough skin (denticles), meat eater, reproduction, some species produce live young, some species lay eggs, dangerous, man eater, attack swimmers, fatal attacks near Pacific coast, 20 kinds attack man

HABITAT — near Florida beaches, Milwaukee restaurants (dolphins), aquariums, sea world

ECONOMIC USES — skin for sandpaper, skin for leather, for vitamins, meat, sport, protect man, killed for

FOOD — eat garbage, eat metal, crabs, squid, shrimp, fish, barnacles

SIZE (Species vary) — ounces to 20 tons, 6 inches to 65 feet

STRUCTURE — small eyes, dorsal fin, jaws with sharp teeth, very tough skin, covered with denticles

SHARKS

Postreading Semantic Map

From *Semantic Mapping: Classroom Applications* (pp. 32–33) by J. E. Heimlich and S. D. Pittelman, 1986, Newark, Del: International Reading Association.

Used as a prereading technique, students can categorize their associations on a topic before reading. A postreading map can be developed that reflects the actual associations and information found in the text. Figure 4.2 is an example of one class's prereading and postreading semantic maps on the topic of sharks.

Other Techniques for Exploring the Relationships Among Ideas in a Passage

Students can be asked to fill in a traditional outline like the following:

Topic sentence: _____

Examples:

   1. _____

   2. _____

   3. _____

The limitation of this format is that it relies on the teacher's visual representation of the text without allowing or requiring students to develop their own. Nonetheless, for beginning students, the prefabricated outline may prove a useful step in the process of having students develop their own sense of the organization of ideas.

- Students can develop their own outline of a paragraph or longer text. While this format may be more familiar to most students than is the semantic map, the latter is certainly worth exploring in contrast to, or together with, traditional outlines.
- Students can generate a list of main ideas from a passage and then work individually or in pairs to locate supporting details.
- Students can be presented with a column of main ideas alongside a column of details. They then work in pairs or groups to match the former with the latter.
- Students might also be asked simply to underline generalizations and supporting details; in the case of implicit arguments, students can create topic sentences for portions of the text. By doing so, students render explicit generalizations for which the text provides support.
- Students can determine the function of each sentence in a paragraph or longer text. These can include not only stating a generalization

and supporting it, but also such functions as catching and holding the reader's attention. Grellet (1981) suggests using a chart format in which students indicate the function of individual sentences:*

	summary of the main point	question to hold the reader's attention	example	anecdote
sentence				
sentence				
sentence				

- Students can choose a main idea (or best title) for a passage from among several choices, or they can create one on their own.
- Students can work together on a jigsaw reading in which students are given different parts of a text, and they must work together to create a logical sequence.

It is important to remember that exploring the relationship of ideas in a text can be carried out at almost any proficiency level. Adolescent and adult students, after all, understand the relationships of ideas; they are simply in the process of developing the skills necessary to recognize these relationships in another language. Beginning-level language students can develop semantic maps that are entirely schematic, containing no writing. For example, a map illustrating an article about a national holiday can contain pictures of flags, food, parades, etc. Similarly, students can match and underline text at any level, or fill in charts indicating the function of sentences within a text.

STRUCTURING A TEXT: INDUCTIVE AND DEDUCTIVE ARGUMENTS

Students can learn to recognize whether an argument is inductive or deductive: whether the author begins with a generalization, which is then supported (**deductive argumentation**), or builds toward a final generalization (**inductive argumentation**).

---

*From *Developing Reading Skills: A Practical Guide to Reading Comprehension Exercises* (p. 93) by F. Grellet, 1981, Cambridge: Cambridge University Press.

Activities

In the following examples, the students' attention is called to the techniques employed by writers to signal paragraph organization.*

1. (Deductive organization)

Large cars cause their owners several problems. First, they cost a lot of money. They are *also* more expensive to run, using twice as much fuel as small cars and producing higher repair bills. *Moreover,* they are less maneuverable and more difficult to park, needing additional space.	topic sentence supporting arguments

2. (Inductive organization)

Many well-paid jobs require some kind of formal academic training. Promotion, *furthermore,* usually comes quicker to those with advanced degrees or professional qualifications. *In addition,* most specialized fields, such as research and the professions, demand higher education of the would-be entrant. Clearly, a university education is an important asset for a young person today.	arguments topic/ concluding sentence

After their introduction to these patterns, students can practice identifying them in other articles and textbooks in their fields.

RECOGNIZING RHETORICAL PATTERNS

Recognizing rhetorical patterns typical of English expository prose can facilitate reading comprehension. In light of cross-cultural research suggesting important differences in rhetorical conventions,[1] it is particularly worthwhile to work with these patterns within a reading program.

> There is, however, a major pitfall in discussions of rhetorical structure: Students may come to expect passages that can be obviously classified within a single rhetorical form. It is important to alert students to the fact that multiple, simultaneous organizational patterns are possible. Similarly, it is important that activities focusing on rhetorical patterns *not* be presented as ancillary to the reading process; such activities should be designed primarily to aid text comprehension.

---

*From *Reading English for Academic Study* (p. 124) by M. H. Long, W. Allen, A. Cyr, C. Pomeroy, E. Ricard, N. Spada, and P. Vogel, 1980, Rowley, Mass: Newbury House.

In the type of EAP class described in our sample lesson, students typically focus on the rhetorical patterns discussed below. Sample activity formats are provided for each pattern. Each is designed to call attention to the relationships among ideas within a reading passage.

Comparison and Contrast

In this organizational scheme, claims are made on the basis of similarities and differences. Some items under discussion are claimed to be similar (compared), while others are shown to be different (contrasted).

Activities

Students locate items being compared and areas of contrast. Here is an example of a passage organized on the basis of comparisons and contrasts:

> The camera and the eye are similar in many respects. They both need light rays in order to function. Both have a sensitive surface on which the image is formed. In the eye the image is formed on the retina. In the camera the image is formed on the film. As in the camera, the image on the retina is inverted.
>
> Both the eye and the camera have a lens. The lens focuses the image on the sensitive surface. In the camera, the lens moves backwards and forwards. In the eye the curvature of the lens is changed. In this respect the eye differs from the camera.
>
> Both the eye and the camera are sensitive to light, shade, and color. The film records light, shade, and color. The eye perceives them but does not record them. The two eyes together produce a three-dimensional image. The camera lens produces a two-dimensional image.

After examining the passage, students could be asked to complete a table like the following and then to compare and contrast the similarities and differences.*

Characteristics	Eye	Camera
The image is inverted		
The lens focuses the image		
Sensitive to light, shade, and color		
Produces three-dimensional image		

*Passage and table adapted from *Reading and Thinking in English: Exploring Functions* (pp. 90–91), Associate Editor H.G. Widdowson, 1979, Oxford: Oxford University Press.

Cause and Effect

Here arguments are made concerning the underlying causes and effects of events. The reader is asked to accept the fact that there is a causal relationship between factors cited and results.

Activities

In typical activities, students identify causes and effects, then evaluate whether the claim(s) for causation prove convincing.

Chronological Order

Some texts are structured on the basis of time. Typically such texts describe events in the order in which they occurred or in reverse chronological order.

Activities

Typical activities are designed to determine whether students have understood a sequence of events. Students can be asked to complete a timeline or otherwise place events in sequence, or they can be asked to correct an incorrect sequence.

Classification

These passages are structured by classifying information on the basis of a hierarchy of categories. For example, a text might outline main subfields of an academic discipline, citing examples of work within each.

Activities

Interpretation of this type of text is often facilitated by visual representation. Students can be asked to complete charts, outlines, or diagrams, or to create their own semantic maps.

Process

These texts describe a process, for example, how to write a book, or build a house, or cook a particular food. This type of organization can overlap substantially with a chronological organizing scheme. Process texts often contain diagrams and illustrations that allow students to practice integrating prose and nonprose information.

Activities

In order to explicate such a passage, students can be asked to reproduce the process or to describe it for someone else who must carry it out.

Definition

Texts and arguments can be built around definitions. In the course of creating a definition, one can create an entire picture of the world. Consider, for example, the variety of definitions and descriptions possible for the word *terrorism*.

Activity

In order to practice gaining information from passages structured around definitions, students can be asked to guess the focus of passages that have had the key term(s) omitted.

STRUCTURING A TEXT: RECOGNIZING GENRE CONVENTIONS

Students of English for academic purposes will likely encounter journal articles in their studies in English. As Huckin and Olsen (1983, pp. 275–276) point out, journal articles may differ in style, but most share a remarkably uniform purpose and structure:

> The purpose of an article in any field is to advance an argument of fact or policy: (1) an argument of fact that the results reported are valid, that previously reported results are supported (or not), that a given theory is supported (or not), that other observations are necessary to resolve some debates in the field; or (2) an argument of policy that previous results should be questioned or reinterpreted, that a given theory should be abandoned, recast, or extended. These arguments are made in a structure that is quite consistent over many fields and includes the following sections:
>
> 1. *Introduction,* which defines the problem and describes its importance
> 2. *Materials and Method,* which describes how the research arrived at the results
> 3. *Results,* which describes what was discovered
> 4. *Discussion,* which analyzes the importance of the results and their implication(s).

Introduction

Huckin and Olsen argue that Introductions tend to introduce a problem, then identify a strategy to address the problem, and announce the purpose of the text. This is accomplished in rather complex and varied ways. They cite Swales' (1981) study of 16 articles each from

physics, biology/medicine, and the social sciences. Notice that in Swales'
structure the presentation of the problem extends into or through his
Move Three.

Figure 4.3. A Possible Structure for Article Introductions

THE FOUR MOVES			NUMBER OF OCCURRENCES IN 48 ARTICLE INTRODUCTIONS
Move One	Establishing the field		43
	A	Showing centrality	25
		i By interest	6
		ii By importance	6
		iii By topic prominence	7
		iv By standard procedure	6
	B	Stating current knowledge	11
	C	Ascribing key characteristics	7
Move Two	Summarizing previous research		48
Move Three	Preparing for present research		40
	A	Indicating a gap	20
	B	Raising questions	14
	C	Extending a finding	6
Move Four	Introducing present research		46
	A	Giving the purpose	23
	B	Describing present research	23

From *Aspects of Article Introductions* (Aston ESP Research Report No. 1, p. 22a) by
J. Swales, 1981, University of Aston, Birmingham, England. Reprinted in *English for
Science and Technology: A Handbook for Nonnative Speakers* (p. 277) by T. N. Huckin
and L.A. Olsen, 1983, New York: McGraw-Hill.

Activities
Students can bring journal articles to class and examine a series of
Introductions. The goal is to develop familiarity with the conventions
of their fields, so that they will be able to better form predictions as
they read. In groups students can work on the following questions:

1. What types of problems are usually posed?
   Are these problems of fact (e.g., problems caused by missing data
   or the difficulty of collecting data) or of policy (e.g., the interpretation
   of data or the development of theory)?
2. Is the literature reviewed?
3. How detailed is the description of the method/strategy used to address the problem?
4. Are the results stated in detail?

Students can also note stylistic conventions: for example, are Introductions brief and technical or are they often designed to catch the reader's attention through use of surprising information or anecdotes?

Students can examine texts to identify the function of each sentence. Figure 4.4 is an example from Huckin and Olsen.

Figure 4.4. Thermal Conductivity and Specific Heat of Epoxy-Resin from 0.1–8.0 K

1 Establishing the field	The thermal properties of glassy materials at low temperatures are still not completely understood. The thermal conductivity has a plateau which is usually in the range of 5 to 10 K, and below this temperature it has a temperature dependence which varies approximately as T^2. The specific heat below 4 K is much larger than that which would be expected from the Debye theory, and it often has an additional term which is proportional to T.
2 Summarizing previous research	Some progress has been made towards understanding the thermal behaviour by assuming that there is a cutoff in the phonon spectrum at high frequencies (Zaitlin and Anderson 1975 a,b) and that there is an additional system of low-lying two level states (Anderson 1975, Phillips 1972).
3 Preparing the present research	Nevertheless, more experimental data are required, and in particular it would seem desirable to make experiments on glassy samples whose properties can be varied slightly from one to the other.
4 Introducing present research	The present investigation reports attempts to do this by using various samples of the same epoxy-resin which have been subjected to different curing cycles. Measurements of the specific heat (or the diffusity) and the thermal conductivity have been taken in the temperature range 0.1 to 8.0 K for a set of specimens which covered up to nine different curing cycles.

From *English for Science and Technology: A Handbook for Nonnative Speakers* (p. 278) by T. N. Huckin and L.A. Olsen, 1983, New York: McGraw-Hill.

Materials and Method

This section provides the means by which the scholarly community can repeat and verify research. Huckin and Olsen argue that this section must:

1. Identify precisely the materials used.

2. Identify any special conditions under which the research was conducted.

3. Identify any special criteria used to select materials.

4. Identify method used to conduct research.

5. Justify, where necessary, choices of criteria, materials, method, or conditions.

Activities
In order to better understand the Materials and Methods sections, students can work in groups or pairs describing to each other procedures that only some of them have read, paying special attention to areas of misunderstanding, either of the text or the speaker.

Results
This section presents the major findings, including a compact presentation of the data (often using charts and graphs), and the major generalizations to be drawn. Students need to become familiar with the fact that prose or nonprose material taken alone can prove incomplete or even uninterpretable.

Activities
Students may need practice integrating prose and nonprose information. The variety of formats presented in Chapter Three can aid in developing skill in this area. In addition, Results sections sometimes lend themselves to a kind of jigsaw reading: One group of students can become "experts" on the nonprose presentation, another on the prose description. These two groups then work together to gain full comprehension of the text. They can continue by evaluating the claims made on the basis of the results.

Discussion
This section of a text claims implications for the Results. Huckin and Olsen note that the following kinds of information appear in the Discussion sections of journal articles:

1. Whether or not the results were expected. If not, why not.

2. Generalizations or claims made on the basis of results.

3. Whether the results contradict or support other experimental results.

4. Whether the results suggest other research to confirm, refute, or extend the current results.

5. Whether the results support or contradict existing theory.

6. Whether the results suggest modifications or extensions of existing theory.

7. Practical applications following from the results.

Activities

It is important for students to evaluate the Discussion sections of journal articles. One activity format has students develop their own Discussion sections before reading the published one. This activity helps ascertain whether students have understood the import of the results, and also whether they will agree with the claims made on the basis of these results.

Of course every essay (or paragraph) does not conform to a single organizational scheme. Recognizing these organizational patterns, however, can help students understand the development of an argument, and perhaps, more importantly, to critique arguments.

EVALUATING ARGUMENTS

Once students understand the structure of an argument they can evaluate it by asking themselves the following types of questions concerning the organizational schemes they encounter.

- **Generalizations with supporting information:** Do examples and illustrations sufficiently support the general claims made?
- **Inductive and deductive arguments:** Is the structure of the argument clear? Once again, do the examples and illustrations sufficiently support the general claims made?
- **Comparison and contrast:** Are the items compared actually similar? Are the contrasts indeed differences? Do these similarities and differences have the effect/import claimed?
- **Cause and effect:** Does the passage adequately demonstrate a causal relationship between factors cited and results?
- **Chronological order:** Are the events mentioned of equal importance? Is strict chronological order violated for any reason? If so, do you find this organization successful?
- **Classification:** Do you accept these as the major categories involved, or do these categories omit important elements of the phenomenon being described? Do you agree with the author's definition of these categories and the choice of examples for each?
- **Process:** Is the description effective? Is sufficient information provided to allow a reader to understand and even duplicate the procedure? (As an example, readers might ask themselves whether they have ever encountered a description of the process of making pop-

corn that would adequately instruct anyone who did not already know how to do so.)

- **Definition:** Is the definition clear? Are readers provided enough information to use the term in question on their own? Are the illustrations persuasive and informative? Do you agree with the definition? Why or why not?
- **Introduction:** Does the introduction adequately define the problem and establish its importance? Is the literature review adequate? Is the current research adequately introduced?
- **Materials and method:** Are the materials and procedures adequately described and justified?
- **Results:** Is the data presented clearly and in enough detail to be explanatory? Do the generalizations clearly follow from the data?
- **Discussion:** Do the claims made follow from the data? Are implications and practical applications convincingly presented?

Students can also critique the overall presentation of ideas. If their expectations are consistently violated, it may be that the author has not presented ideas logically. Through a developing familiarity with the conventions of expository prose, students can come to trust their instincts and their evaluations of texts.

Other elements of evaluating texts are presented in the following chapter, "Editorializing and Opinion."

GRAMMATICAL/LEXICAL FEATURES

Rhetorical Markers

Grammatical/lexical features can often signal the rhetorical organizations outlined above.[2] For a native speaker, the appearance of these features can immediately suggest specific organizational strategies. Nonnative speakers can be helped to recognize the markers listed below.

Some are presented here with a strong cautionary note. It is never advisable to present students with uncontextualized lists. It is best to call students' attention to these markers as they are encountered in the students' texts and when they significantly impact text structure and comprehensibility.

- **Comparison and contrast:** *like, both, same, similar, comparable, parallel, in the same way, once again, however, although, but, yet, whereas, in fact, on the other hand, on the contrary, notwithstanding, unlike, even so, is different from, differs from, in contrast, instead, though, nevertheless, nonetheless, in spite of this*
- **Cause and effect:** *consequently, as a result, cause, effect, therefore, leads to, yields, for this reason, thus, because, since, so long as, in turn, accordingly, finally, and so, and that is why*
- **Classification:** *types, kinds, subset, major, method, part, division, types, qualities, aspects, characteristics, factors, classes, categories, (un)important, (in)significant, fundamental*
- **Chronology:** *after, presently, before, meanwhile, immediately, following this, the next day, soon afterward, afterward, by that time, after that, next, while, later, soon, when, at last, shortly, earlier, at that moment, from then on, then*
- **Process:** *first, second, finally, when, then, as soon as, the latter, next, while, during, become*
- **Definition:** *kind, form, species, category, device, characteristic, aspect, method, property, define, clarify, explain, paraphrase, attribute.*

Activity
As students identify and work with the rhetorical structure of passages encountered in their texts, they can be asked to note rhetorical markers and to decide what function specific markers fulfill.

Verbs
Choice of verb tense, aspect, or voice carries important information in English. Huckin and Olsen (1983, p. 441) argue that "of the 12 traditional verb tenses in English, only five are used with any frequency in scientific and technical writing: simple present, simple past, present perfect, present progressive, and future (*will*)." Students need to be able to recognize the common uses of these tenses in the readings they encounter. Below is a brief description of verb choice in scientific and technical English; the discussion of the five most common tenses is based primarily on Huckin and Olsen.

The simple present. In formal scientific and technical English, the simple present is used primarily to express "timeless" generalizations, for example, the statement, "Water freezes at 0°C."

The simple past. The simple past specifies a particular event or condition that occurred or existed at some point in the past but no longer occurs/exists. For example, procedures in an experiment are usually described in the simple past, as are the immediate results of these procedures.

The present perfect. Whereas the simple past tense is used to describe events completed in the past, the present perfect is used for actions that were begun in the past but remain ongoing. In a review of the literature, an author might refer to an isolated study in the simple past, but refer to a study that is part of a current research question in the present perfect; for example, "Smith and others have noted that...."
The present perfect tense is also used to report actions that were carried out in the past but are still producing effects in the present. Huckin and Olsen provide this example taken from the opening paragraph of a company memo:

> Our patent department lawyers *have asked* this research group to provide them with data for a patent infringement suit. A competitor *has* recently *marketed* a new tower packing which they claim has superior pressure drop characteristics compared to our product (p. 443).

The use of the present perfect tense in the first sentence indicates that the lawyers' request remains in effect. The use of the present perfect in the second sentence implies that the efforts to market the product are active. Huckin and Olsen summarize: "The choice of the present perfect tense in both cases thus serves to emphasize the immediate ongoing nature of the threat posed by the competitor's past actions" (p. 443).

The present progressive. This verb form is used to describe events that are in the process of occurring. Huckin and Olsen note that it is particularly appropriate to progress reports, letters, and introductions to technical reports. As an example, they cite the following from an introduction to a technical report about electric hybrid vehicles, "Global Design Corporation *is* currently *developing* a computer-controlled vehicle that uses both an internal combustion engine and lead-acid batteries as power sources" (p. 446).

Future (*will*). Often called **modal verb** or **modal auxiliary,** it implies logical necessity. It is used to make strong claims or predictions, for example, "As a result of these findings, we *will* now be able to better understand the fluctuations in the orbit of this star." (Modal auxiliaries are discussed below.)

The passive. The passive voice is used to emphasize the receiver of an action, for example, "In evaluating the bank, particular attention *was focused* on its real estate loans." The passive voice is also used to describe common procedures, for example, "X *is/may be defined* as a function of Y."

Activities
Because verb tenses can carry a good deal of information and are fairly conventionalized in expository prose, students can practice recognizing the functions of verb tense choice through the following types of activities:

- When students predict content during the reading process, they can identify the role that tense choice played in their predictions.
- Students can also note differences in meaning when the same passage is presented in different tenses.
- Finally, as a comprehension measure, students can simply be asked to note the function of tense choice in succeeding parts of the text.

> It is important to remember, however, that it is not worthwhile for students to spend time explicating the language use of a passage that they have already understood perfectly well. Students do not need to become experts in the metalanguage of discourse analysis.

Qualification: Modal Auxiliaries
It is important to recognize the strength of claims made by an author. Have conclusions, suggestions, predictions appeared without qualification, or have the authors modified their claims? Students can be introduced to uses of modal auxiliaries typical of academic prose:*

1. Reporting conclusions.

Will—generalizations	Conclusions that hold in all cases; very strong
May—qualified generalization	Conclusions that hold in some cases; less strong
May—uncertain conclusions	Conclusions of which the author is uncertain; even less strong

---

*Presentation of modal auxiliaries from *Teaching International Undergraduate Science and Social Science Students to Write Experimental Research Papers* by M. Ellis, 1989, unpublished manuscript, University of Washington, Seattle. Research based on Huddelston (1971); and Hanania and Akhtar (1985).

2. Making predictions.

Will—strong prediction	**Things that will surely happen; very strong**
May—weaker prediction	**Things that the author thinks may happen; less strong**

3. Making suggestions.

Must—obligation	**A very strong suggestion**
Should—advice	**A less strong suggestion**

4. Making predictions based on previous actions.
Would—Strong hypothetical prediction
Should—A less strong suggestion

Examples:

The incidence of severe lung disease in Winnipeg *may* increase in the next 10 years.

An increase in lung disease in Winnipeg *will* result in higher taxes.

Major changes *should* be made in the St. Louis antipollution laws in order to reduce the incidence of emphysema.

Activity

Students can then examine a passage such as the one below for the use of stronger and weaker modifiers. The passage is taken from the *Journal of Finance.**

We have focused solely on interest rate risk and have said nothing concerning the important role of credit risk. Our feeling is that credit risk will have an asymmetric influence on the maturity intermediation decisions of intermediaries. For institutions where high interest rates correspond to lower profits, credit risk will tend to reduce its demand for long-term borrowing. Moreover, for firms where low-rate environments result in lower profits, credit risk may also cause the demand for long-term borrowing to be higher. However, a complete multi-period analysis of investment and financing decision with credit and interest rate risk awaits future research efforts.

---

*From "Maturity Intermediation" by G.E. Morgan and S.D. Smith, 1987, *Journal of Finance,* 4, p. 1033. Quoted in *Teaching International Undergraduate Science and Social Science Students to Write Experimental Research Papers,* by M. Ellis, 1989, unpublished manuscript, University of Washington, Seattle.

Qualification: Other Devices

Other devices for modification can also be introduced. Here is a sample introduction along with a practice reading exercise:*

Some common ways of preceding a generalization with a modification or qualification are shown below. This is not an exhaustive list.

1. *Although* 1975 was a poor year, all four areas have had above average harvests for the region during the last decade.
2. *While* its education policy was occasionally problematic, the government's term of office was considered highly successful.
3. *Even though* differing in the strength of the relationship they have found, all the studies reported have shown a relationship between socioeconomic status and educational achievement.
4. *Despite* declining sales in recent years, the company continues to hold a major share of the market.
4a. *Despite the fact that* its sales have declined in recent years, the company continues to hold a major share of the market.
5. *In spite of* a temporary recession in the early part of 1974, the decade was one of rapid economic growth.
5a. *In spite of the fact that* there was a temporary recession in the early part of 1974, the decade was one of rapid economic growth.

Activity

Directions: Match the sentences in Columns A and B below.† Write the letter corresponding to the second part of each idea in the parentheses beside each number. The first item serves as an example.

A	B
1. (*d*) Even though prices have risen sharply,	a. the proposed legislation was generally well-received.
2. ( ) It is an interesting theory.	b. although some progress has recently been reported.
3. ( ) While rather expensive,	

(continued)

---

*Adapted from *Reading English for Academic Study* (p. 142) by M.H. Long, W. Allen, A. Cyr, C. Pomeroy, E. Ricard, N. Spada, and P. Bogel, 1980, Rowley, Mass.: Newbury House.

†Adapted from *Reading English for Academic Study* (p. 143) by M.H. Long, W. Allen, A. Cyr, C. Pomeroy, E. Ricard, N. Spada and P. Bogel, 1980, Rowley, Mass.: Newbury House.

A	B

4. ( ) In spite of the fact that
some criticisms were
made,

5. ( ) The animals are
herbivorous.

6. ( ) Causes of the disease are
still unknown,

7. ( ) Millions of people still
smoke cigarettes,

8. ( ) There is still an urgent
need for additional
funding,

c. However, it is not fully specified
in some areas.

d. consumer spending is still high.

e. it is the best available.

f. Nevertheless, a few cases of
preying on small rodents have
been reported.

g. in spite of an increase in
government support for the
program.

h. despite a fall in numbers in
recent years.

To complete this exercise efficiently, students must make a series of fairly precise linguistic predictions based on their knowledge of syntax and rhetorical conventions.

Reference

Cohesive devices link otherwise independent sentences thereby creating texts. A powerful cohesive device is the use of repeated references to a thing or concept. If students are unable to recognize these links, serious misunderstandings can result. One goal of a reading program can be to help students recognize and interpret reference devices. Huckin and Olsen (1983) document the following cohesive devices:

1. Repeating a noun or noun phrase exactly from one sentence to another.

> *Example: The proposed system* meets all of the criteria specified by the design team: *The proposed system* is compact enough to fit into a 4' × 5' area and is economically competitive. (p. 408)

2. Repeating a shortened form of a noun phrase.

> *Example:* Electric cars must be able to meet *the same safety standards that gasoline cars must meet* as set up by the Department of Transportation. *These standards* are derived from an established crash test, in which the car is propelled against a solid wall at 30 mph. (p. 409)

3. Using noun compounds.

> *Example:* This low worker productivity has caused the *backlog of active and "waiting" requests* to rise above 2,000 requests. Simply having this large a *backlog size* causes excessive processing delays. (p. 417)

4. Using pronouns, articles, and demonstratives.

> *Example:* As the months go by, *the experiences of physicians who are testing the substance* will be published in medical journals and collected by the Federal Drug Administration. When *these* appear positive and consistent with the results obtained in Europe, *it* will be approved for use for ordinary patients who might benefit from *it* in any way.

5. Using a synonym.

> *Example: The population problem* in the world cannot be solved with one 5-year plan, or in a single decade. But the time is late and *the task* immense.

6. Using a noun phrase very closely associated with an earlier noun phrase (repetition of associated terms).

> *Example: The theoretical deflection of the edge members under the live load* was calculated to be .027 in., whereas *the actual deflection* was .025 in. *The structural strength of the building* was thus shown not to have been impaired by the fire. (pp. 425–426)

Activity

At the intermediate levels of language proficiency, nonnative speakers seem to have most trouble with devices listed under Item 4 above. Only if these devices prove an obstacle to understanding should students be provided practice in identifying referents. Here is an activity developed by Grellet (1981). The instructor introduces the distinction between references that refer to something already mentioned (**anaphora**) and those that refer to something that is going to be mentioned (**cataphora**). Students read a passage, then complete the chart that follows.

Directions: In the following passage all of the italicized words refer to something mentioned before, or after, in the text. Read the passage carefully and complete the chart (figure 4.5).

> The idea of evolution (*which* is gradual change) was not a new *one*. The Greeks had thought of *it*, so had Erasmus Darwin, the grandfather of Charles, and also the Frenchman, Lamarck. *It* is one thing to have an idea; we can all of us guess and sometimes make a lucky guess. *It* is quite another thing to produce a proof of the correctness of that idea. Darwin thought he had *that* proof in *his* notebooks. *He* saw that all animals had a struggle to survive. *Those* which were best at surviving *their* environment passed on the good qualities which had helped *them* to *their* descendants. *This* was called "the survival of the fittest." For

example, in a cold climate, *those* who have the warmest fur will live. Darwin believed that *this* necessity for an animal to deal with *its* environment explained the immense variety of creatures.

Figure 4.5. Reference Chart

| | refers to something | | what it refers to |
	before	after	
which	x		*the idea of evolution*
one	x		*idea*
it	x		*the idea of evolution*
It		x	*to have an idea*
Now go on!			
It			
that			
his			
He			
Those			
their			
them			
their			
This			
those			
this			
its			

From *Developing Reading Skills: A Practical Guide to Reading Comprehension Exercises* (pp. 45–46) by F. Grellet, 1981, Cambridge: Cambridge University Press. (Passage reprinted from *Britain and the World* by A. M. Newth, 1966, Penguin.)

INTEGRATING READING AND WRITING INSTRUCTION

Particularly in EAP contexts, reading and writing instruction benefit from an integrated approach.[3] From one perspective, students read to gain information about which they will write. Students come to recognize written conventions both for the purposes of comprehension and in order to reproduce these in their own writing. More importantly, however, Zamel (1992) argues for "writing one's way into reading." By fully integrating reading and writing instruction, students come to understand the ways in which both readers and writers compose text.

Many of the formats cited above can be altered to accommodate writing instruction by substituting students' own writing for the prepared texts of others. If students are to become independent language users, they must develop the ability to evaluate their own writing.

SUMMARY

Students can become more efficient interpreters of English expository prose by becoming more familiar with the conventions that govern these texts. To practice comprehension of these patterns, students can complete tasks that demonstrate that they have understood the relationship of ideas within a text. These activities can include filling in diagrams (outlines, tree diagrams, or charts), creating semantic maps, underlining parts of a text, or indicating in the margins the functions of particular parts of a passage. Students can also demonstrate comprehension in a less text-based fashion, for example, by recreating a process they have read about.

It is important to note that the goal of these activities is to enhance the comprehending process, both by helping students solve immediate comprehension problems and by providing learners with information about the language patterns and conventions they will encounter in texts. The following are areas that can be explored by students and teachers interpreting English expository prose:

How arguments are structured:

- Generalizations and supporting information
- Inductive and deductive arguments
- Rhetorical patterns
- Genre conventions

Grammatical/lexical features:

- Rhetorical markers
- Verb use
- Qualification
- Reference

·ACTIVITIES·

1. **a.** Choose a piece of academic writing of a kind that your students might encounter. Which categories of activities outlined in this chapter could be applied using this single text?
   b. Which of these activities should be eliminated if evaluated only in terms of whether they illuminated presumed comprehension problems?
   c. Among those you listed for Item 1b above, do other considerations recommend use of some of these activities?

2. Create a semantic map for a passage from this book or from a text you have studied. Do you find this an effective way to summarize text?

3. Create a jigsaw reading activity.

4. Examine a technical text.
   a. Determine the extent to which it
   - contains the sections described by Huckin and Olsen (pp. 57 above),
   - maintains the organization outlined by Swales (p. 58 above).
   b. How might students go about evaluating the claims made in this text?

5. Examine the Introductions to a series of journal articles from a single field. In terms of style, content, and grammatical elements, what features seem to characterize these Introductions? The following are questions you might ask yourself:
   - Do the articles assume an informed audience or a general audience?
   - Do the articles use anecdotes or other devices to catch readers' attention?
   - What information seems to appear in most of the Introductions; what questions are answered?

- What verb choices seem consistent: Passive voice? Present tense?
- Are any organizational patterns typical: Deductive vs. inductive organization? Cause and effect rhetorical structures?

6. Develop an activity that provides students practice in predicting subsequent text.

Notes

[1]For an overview of work in contrastive rhetoric, see Leki (1991).

[2]For a comprehensive discussion of second language grammar instruction, see Celce-Murcia and Hillis (1988), *Techniques and Resources in Teaching Grammar* in this series.

[3]For a comprehensive discussion of second language writing instruction, see Raimes (1983), *Techniques in Teaching Writing* in this series.

·CHAPTER FIVE·
EDITORIALIZING AND OPINION

Bringing editorials and opinion pieces into the second language classroom is an excellent way to practice critical reading skills. Perhaps even more effective, however, is to use such pieces to help students recognize the limitations on objectivity inherent in any text. For some students, developing these skills can prove a special challenge. They may be unfamiliar with a critical examination of texts that searches for philosophical presuppositions and underlying points of view. These same students may be unsettled by the notion that there is no uniquely appropriate reader response and no single "correct" interpretation of a text. This unfamiliarity renders student initiative and participation particularly important in critical reading activities.

SAMPLE LESSON

We are in an academic English class. Students of the natural sciences have been researching the topic of AIDS. Currently, they are examining the single-topic issue of *Scientific American* (October 1988) titled *What Science Knows About AIDS*.

EXAMINING THE FUNCTION OF WRITING

Students begin by brainstorming the functions of prose. They decide that they will develop a provisional list to be revised after they have examined sections of the magazine. Here is their initial list.

Functions of Prose:

to persuade	to anger
to inform	to please
to entertain	

The students' first task is to determine the function of different parts of the magazine. They begin by examining the table of contents. The title of each full-length article is followed by a short descriptive paragraph. Here is the first:

AIDS in 1988
Robert C. Gallo and Luc Montagnier

Where do we stand? What are the key areas of current research? The prospects for therapy or a vaccine? In their first collaborative article the two investigators who established the cause of AIDS answer these questions and tell how HIV was isolated and linked to AIDS.

Students begin by puzzling over the function of this short text. Is it only to inform readers what will be contained in the article? Looking sentence by sentence, students discover that small parts of text can maintain different functions:

Where do we stand? Students agree that if the sole purpose of this sentence were to inform, they would expect to see a declaratory sentence such as, "This article describes the current medical understanding of AIDS." Instead, the question construction in this and the next two sentences seems designed to intrigue the reader, to develop interest in reading the article. Students turn their attention to the last sentence in the table of contents description.

In their first collaborative article the two investigators who established the cause of AIDS answer these questions and tell how HIV was isolated and linked to AIDS. The students note that this sentence too seems designed to intrigue: The two people who discovered the HIV virus (this also establishes their credibility) are writing together for the first time (and the reader is given the opportunity to read this state-of-the-art account). Students also note the detective story quality of this sentence: The authors will describe the discovery process for the AIDS virus.

Students note that the function of entire texts is enhanced by the function of the parts of a text. A table of contents squib, designed in part to inform, carries out its various other functions (to intrigue, to invite further reading) through the workings of its subparts.

Students confirm their sense of the function and tone of this first bit of text (somewhat like an advertisement for the articles) by contrasting it to a short description of the cover photo:

THE COVER of this single-topic issue of SCIENTIFIC AMERICAN shows a particle of the human immunodeficiency virus (HIV) forming at the outer membrane of an infected cell. (The new particle is the circular form at the upper right.) HIV, the AIDS virus, can enter a cell and remain latent until it is activated to make new viral components. The particles then self-assemble in the process depicted on the cover. HIV causes a broad spectrum of diseases of which AIDS is only the culmination.

Comparing the technical approach of this descriptive paragraph to that of the table of contents paragraph examined first, it seems clear that this paragraph serves a very different function. This paragraph seems largely designed to inform, with individual sentences serving to elaborate and describe. However, the students do not stop here. One student notes that the technical language of the paragraph announces that this is not a magazine addressed to the general reader. Another student complains that the attempt at description is disingenuous. After all, what is a *viral component* and what does it mean to *self-assemble*? This student wonders if one function of this paragraph is to announce that science is technical and not really available to any but a very few. He argues that this "popular" science magazine may serve, in fact, to mythologize science, to obscure and confuse, thus maintaining the role and status of the scientist. The class begins to suspect that, not only do texts have multiple functions, but that there may be no texts, even among technical reports, that do not contain a point of view, an opinion, that do not editorialize.

   The students agree that the next class session should focus on extended prose and decide to examine the article by Robert C. Gallo and Luc Montagnier described in the table of contents.

   The students begin by examining the title and epigraph:

AIDS in 1988

In their first collaborative article the investigators who discovered HIV introduce a single-topic issue on AIDS. They recount the discovery and offer prospects for vaccine, for therapy and for the epidemic.

by Robert C. Gallo and Luc Montagnier

   The students puzzle over the fact that the title of the article is not technical. One student argues that a magazine with the title *Scientific American* should title its articles more "scientifically." Another student points out that this seems to be a magazine that popularizes science. The title seems to advertise information as would a title like, "Everything you Need to Know about AIDS in 1988." Students also note similarities and differences between the table of contents squib and the epigraph. In the former, the authors will *tell* how AIDS was discovered; the epigraph announces that they will *recount* the discovery—emphasizing the storytelling/narrative potential of the tale.

RECOGNIZING PRESUPPOSITIONS/ DRAWING INFERENCES

The students move on to examine the opening paragraph:

> As recently as a decade ago it was widely believed that infectious disease was no longer much of a threat in the developed world. The remaining challenges to public health there, it was thought, stemmed from noninfectious conditions such as cancer, heart disease and degenerative diseases. That confidence was shattered in the early 1980's by the advent of AIDS. Here was a devastating disease caused by a class of infectious agents—retroviruses—that had first been found in human beings only a few years before. In spite of the startling nature of the epidemic, science responded quickly. In the two years from mid–1982 to mid–1984 the outlines of the epidemic were clarified, a new virus—the human immunodeficiency virus (HIV)—was isolated and was shown to cause the disease, a blood test was formulated and the virus's targets in the body were established.

Again the students feel that this is not a form of "neutral" scientific prose. Students begin to focus on presuppositions and inferences, those unstated assumptions and ideologies incorporated into a text. Again, they move sentence by sentence, this time seeking unstated assumptions. *As recently as a decade ago it was widely believed that infectious disease was no longer much of a threat in the developed world*: Among other things, this sentence presupposes that a decade is a relatively short period of time, and that what was once believed about infectious diseases is no longer believed.

The remaining challenges to public health there, it was thought, stemmed from noninfectious conditions such as cancer, heart disease and degenerative diseases: Again, what is unstated but presupposed is that what "was thought" is no longer believed. Without stating it explicitly, the authors announce that they are setting up a straw person. What was once widely believed is no longer the case.

We know that very recently we misunderstood our public health context. We are told in the next two sentences that AIDS, a *devastating* and *startling epidemic, shattered confidence.* Into this breach of mis-understanding and shock steps big science to the rescue: *science re-sponded quickly.* If a decade is a relatively short period of time, we can infer that the authors find it remarkable that a mere two years (from mid-1982 to mid-1984) was needed to (a) clarify the outlines of the epidemic, (b) isolate a new virus, (c) demonstrate that the virus caused the disease, (d) develop a blood test, and (e) establish the virus's targets in the body.

The students return to their task of discerning the function(s) of the text. They brainstorm functions of this initial paragraph including creating an urgent historical context for this article and establishing the credentials of big science. Some students feel that by establishing the credentials of science, the authors establish their personal creden-tials as primary players in the current drama.

The second paragraph seems to take a different tack, but students begin to feel more confident and justified in their inferences concerning the function of the article and the authors' point of view:

> Following that initial burst, progress has been steady, albeit slower. Yet in some respects the virus has outpaced science. No cure or vaccine is yet available, and the epidemic continues to spread; disease-causing retroviruses will be among the human population for a long time. In view of that prospect, it is essential to ask where we stand in relation to AIDS in 1988. How was HIV discovered and linked to AIDS? How does the virus cause its devastation? What are the chances that AIDS will spread rapidly outside the known high-risk groups? What are the prospects for a vaccine? For therapy? How can the epidemic most ef-fectively be fought? Those are some of the questions this article and this issue of *Scientific American* have set out to answer.

This second paragraph seems designed to lower expectations, but the students infer that science is still in charge. *Progress has been steady*—in some respects only has the virus outpaced science. The list of difficult questions that remain are defined by and remain within the realm to which science can respond. Students find the final sentence particularly intriguing: *Those are some of the questions this article and this issue of* Scientific American *have set out to answer.*

Like the table of contents and the epigraph, the sentence announces future content and invites further reading. Students wonder if the choice of words is significant. *Scientific American* does not answer these questions; rather it *sets out to answer* these questions. One student believes that this presupposes a difficult process that has only begun, as though one were setting out on a journey. Another student wonders if we are to infer that *Scientific American* tackles difficult and important tasks. A student wonders to what extent the information in this segment is fact or opinion.

DISTINGUISHING FACT FROM OPINION

Examining the first sentence of the paragraph reproduced above, students debate whether it is fact or opinion that *progress has been steady*. They note that activist groups argue that progress has been too slow, and not steady. Fact and opinion, then, depend both on the assumptions of the reader and also on the data provided in the text. Presumably the lengthy scientific discussions to follow provide some evidence of progress. But the pace of the progress seems to be the opinion of the authors. Students examine this paragraph looking for other examples of opinion. One student suggests the statement *disease-causing retroviruses will be among the human population for a long time*. Another student argues that at the current rate of progress we *will* have retroviruses among us for a long time. The first student responds that she thinks a quick cure is possible. The students agree that they cannot know if this statement is true or not based on the text. Weary of the seeming editorializing of this article, the students hope for more straightforward prose in the next paragraph.

RECOGNIZING AN INTENDED AUDIENCE AND POINT OF VIEW

Like other viruses, retroviruses cannot replicate without taking over the biosynthetic apparatus of a cell and exploiting it for their own ends. What is unique about retroviruses is their capacity to reverse the ordinary flow of genetic information—from DNA to RNA to proteins (which are the cell's structural and functional molecules). The genetic material of a retrovirus is RNA. In addition, the retrovirus carries an enzyme called reverse transcriptase, which can use the viral RNA as a template for making DNA. The viral DNA can integrate itself into the genome (the complement of genetic information) of the host. Having made itself at home among the host's genes, the viral DNA remains latent until it is activated to make new virus particles. The latent DNA can also initiate the process that leads to tumor formation.

The students focus first on the intended audience of this piece of prose. Their reactions are divided. Some feel that the introduction invites any intelligent reader; others feel that only someone with considerable previous technical knowledge could follow this paragraph and the remainder of the article. As evidence of required prior knowledge, students point to phrases that refer to the ordinary situation (very thinly described) from which retroviruses differ, phrases such as *like other viruses,* and *the ordinary flow of genetic information.* Once again the suggestion is made that this type of scientific writing—writing that pretends to invite the uninformed, without commitment to full description—serves only to reinforce the notion that science is not within the grasp of the general public. Members of the class disagree whether this type of article is explicitly designed to empower the scientist at the expense of the general public. At this level, debates about intention and function are not easily resolved.

The students also note that the metaphors around which this description is built are not explicitly "scientific." The paragraph is framed using the language of colonialism that seems to ascribe an almost human agency to retroviruses: retroviruses *take over* the biosynthetic apparatus of a cell and *exploit* it for *their own ends.* The teacher wonders aloud if this scientific description would be written differently in another part of the world.

The students begin to suspect that it is impossible to write without a point of view, without an opinion, without editorializing. They further suspect that all texts assume an audience and take a turn in a specific "conversation," with its own context and assumptions. In fact, they add to their list of textual functions those of announcing and recreating a community of readers. The next week students will bring to class a text from their specific fields and define the audience, the presuppositions, and the context. For the next class meeting, however, they decide to look at a piece of prose with a more explicit point of view and to discuss the process of evaluation.

EVALUATING A POINT OF VIEW

The next day students read the advertisement for smokers' rights reproduced in figure 5.1.

Figure 5.1. Advertisement for Smokers' Rights

Smoking in Public: Live and Let Live

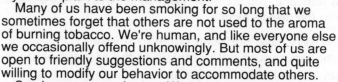

Ours is a big world, complex and full of many diverse people. People with many varying points of view are constantly running up against others who have differing opinions. Those of us who smoke are just one group of many. Recently, the activism of non-smokers has reminded us of the need to be considerate of others when we smoke in public.

But, please! Enough is enough! We would like to remind non-smokers that courtesy is a two-way street. If you politely request that someone not smoke you are more likely to receive a cooperative response than if you scowl fiercely and hurl insults. If you speak directly to someone, you are more likely to get what you want than if you complain to the management.

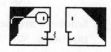

Many of us have been smoking for so long that we sometimes forget that others are not used to the aroma of burning tobacco. We're human, and like everyone else we occasionally offend unknowingly. But most of us are open to friendly suggestions and comments, and quite willing to modify our behavior to accommodate others.

Smokers are people, too. We laugh and cry. We have hopes, dreams, aspirations. We have children, and mothers, and pets. We eat our hamburgers with everything on them and salute the flag at Fourth of July picnics. We hope you'll remember that the next time a smoker lights up in public.

Just a friendly reminder from your local Smokers Rights Association.

From: *Reader's Choice* (2nd ed., p. 82) by E. M. Baudoin, E. S. Bober, M. A. Clarke, B. K. Dobson, and S. Silberstein, 1988, Ann Arbor, Mich.: University of Michigan Press.

First, students are asked to identify the presuppositions and point of view. Then, in a lively discussion, students evaluate the views expressed. The focus of the teacher-prepared activities below is on probing the perspective of the author, then comparing it with the reader's perspective before and after reading. Some of the items below are designed for debate and do not have a single correct response set.

Recognizing the Point of View

This exercise should be completed after reading "Smoking in Public: Live and Let Live."

Directions: Below you will find portions of the editorial, followed by a list of statements. Put a check (√) next to each of the statements that reflects the underlying beliefs or point of view of the original text.

1. Ours is a big world, complex and full of many diverse people. People with many varying points of view are constantly running up against others who have differing opinions. Those of us who smoke are just one group of many.

_____ a. Smokers are simply another minority in the U.S., such as Greek Americans.

_____ b. Smoking can be thought of as a point of view rather than as a behavior.

_____ c. People should like smokers.

_____ d. Smokers are people, too.

2. We would like to remind nonsmokers that courtesy is a two-way street. If you politely request that someone not smoke, you are more likely to receive a cooperative response than if you scowl fiercely and hurl insults. If you speak directly to someone, you are more likely to get what you want than if you complain to the management.

_____ a. Nonsmokers have not been polite to smokers.

_____ b. Nonsmokers should not complain to the management.

_____ c. Smokers have been uncooperative.

_____ d. If nonsmokers were not so impolite, smokers would be more cooperative.

3. Smokers are people, too. We laugh and cry. We have hopes, dreams, aspirations. We have children, and mothers, and pets.... We hope you'll remember that the next time a smoker lights up in public.

_____ a. Smokers are not always treated like people.

_____ b. Nonsmokers should be nicer to smokers because they have mothers.

_____ c. We should remember smokers' mothers when they light up in public.

_____ d. Having a pet makes you a nice person.

Evaluating a Point of View

1. *Directions*: Check (√) all of the following that are assumptions of this passage.

_____ Secondary smoking (being near people who smoke) can kill you.

———— A major reason smokers are uncooperative is that nonsmokers are not polite.

———— Smokers are people, too.

2. Now look at the statements listed under Item 1 above. This time, check all those with which you agree.

Class Discussion

1. Do you agree with the presuppositions and point of view of this editorial?
2. Is this the same opinion you had before you read the text?
3. What do you think made the passage persuasive?
4. Unpersuasive?

DISCUSSION OF THE LESSON

As in our previous lessons, students worked on texts that were relevant to their needs and interests. The instructor provided opportunities for students to discover the reading process—sometimes participating in a task-based approach, sometimes intervening to supply exercises and activities that provide practice and develop explicit awareness.

By probing the assumptions and world view implicit in texts, students can also explore their own, sometimes unconscious, assumptions. Interrogating an author's point of view, students examine the preconceptions with which they approach texts. This rich interaction of ideas is part of a successful reading process.

EXAMPLES FROM LOWER PROFICIENCY LEVELS

Note that at any proficiency level, students can benefit from activities that allow them to discover the functions of texts, the underlying presuppositions and points of view of texts, and their own evaluation of these. Recent immigrants with limited English, for example, can benefit from examining leases or childcare agreements. Here are sample terms from a lease:

1. Tenants must pay their rent on time. A late fee will be charged.
2. Tenants must tell the rental company immediately if any appliances break.
3. Tenants may not have people live with them who are not listed on the lease.

4. No motorcycles may be stored in the building.
5. No loud noises permitted after 10:00 at night.
6. Cars parked illegally will be towed.

Examining the Function of Writing

Students can **debate** the function of this rental agreement: Is it intended to protect the tenant? the landlord? Is the function of this lease to make responsibilities clear? Whose responsibilities are explained? Does this text have multiple functions? Do different leases seem to have different functions?

Recognizing Presuppositions/Drawing Inferences

In examining presuppositions, students might find themselves exploring assumptions about tenants in general and about previous tenants in this building. Students can explore such issues as: What problems is this rental agreement trying to avoid? Why do you think this is the case? What kind of people would be happy in this building? Who would not be happy?

Distinguishing Fact from Opinion

In some ways this is a difficult text to use to talk about fact and opinion. However, the underlying presuppositions can be explored from this perspective: Are tenants noisy? Do they need to be told to be quiet? Is it important that noise restrictions be placed in leases? Students can debate whether the presuppositions identified here and above are fact or opinion.

Recognizing an Intended Audience and Point of View

Questions that can be explored here are: For whom is this written: the tenant, the landlord, and/or the legal system? What are the implied points of view about tenants? the legal system?

Evaluating a Point of View

Finally, students can evaluate how they feel about what they see as the point of view. For example, some students may feel that leases are necessary to avoid later misunderstanding. Others may find the type of rental agreement presented above to be coercive and unreasonable.

Integrating Reading and Writing

An integrated task might involve rewriting the rental agreement from the tenant's point of view, recasting the given content and adding new responsibilities for the owner.

At any proficiency level, examining and evaluating these elements of a text will generally lead to discussions of one's own point of view and the assumptions with which one approaches and evaluates texts. This evaluation may occur in the course of informal discussion or through the use of more structured formats such as **debates**, **role plays**, or even **simulated press conferences**, in which students portray speakers representing varied perspectives addressed in the reading passage(s).

SUMMARY

All texts have embedded within them implicitly and explicitly signaled presuppositions about the world. Some passages, such as editorials, explicitly state a point of view. Others, for example, technical texts, may make more claims to objectivity. At all proficiency levels, students can benefit from practice in discovering the functions of and perspectives taken by texts along with their own reactions to these.

Examining the function of writing.   The way a text actually functions can be quite different from its announced function. Rental agreements, for example, theoretically designed to protect tenant and renter with a legally explicit understanding, can in fact serve to confuse, intimidate, or disenfranchise. One way to arrange texts is by degree of explicitness. Students can begin with editorials and move to supposedly neutral texts, or vice versa. History texts are particularly rich examples of ideology masquerading as objectivity.

Recognizing presuppositions/drawing inferences.   Practicing these skills can begin on the sentence level and proceed to the examination of entire texts. The ability to draw inferences from text is fundamental to critical reading. Exploring the presuppositions of author and text allows an examination of those of the reader.

Distinguishing fact from opinion.   It is possible to be overly impressed by the authority of written text, particularly in a second language. Opinions are not always explicitly signaled, but the ability to distinguish fact from opinion (often masquerading as fact) is fundamental to reading comprehension.

Recognizing an intended audience and point of view.   Recognizing a community of readers for whom a text is intended is an important part of reading comprehension. There are many textual markers of discourse community. Students can learn both to recognize these and to become part of multiple communities. This will aid readers in recognizing the point of view, often implicitly signaled within a text.

Evaluating a point of view.   Once readers feel confident that they understand the perspective presented in a text, they can evaluate this viewpoint. Each reader's unique evaluation of a text constitutes an important aspect of comprehension. One technique that practices understanding and evaluating perspectives is through the use of written debates. Groups of students can read passages arguing opposing viewpoints. Their first task is to fully explain the point of view of each perspective to the satisfaction of classmates who have not read another perspective. Students then debate and evaluate.

Note that for some students, examining and evaluating the ideological perspectives of texts may initially prove an uncomfortable activity. Some students will come from educational and political systems where this would be a dangerous and/or foolish activity. *Teachers must know their students and exercise discretion in all decisions concerning how students will spend their instructional time.*

1. Here is a sample agreement that must be signed in order to register a child at a daycare center. As you read this text, what seem to be the presuppositions and world view that underlie this text?

  a. A nonrefundable fee must be paid at the time of registration.

  b. Parents cannot register children for the following year if they owe the center money.

  c. A fine will be charged for forgetting to sign your child in or out of the center.

  d. Parents may increase their child's hours at any time, but not decrease them.

  e. Parents must volunteer for 10 hours of work each year.

  f. Parents must give the center 30 days' notice if they are going to withdraw a child from the center.

How might you use this in an ESOL classroom?

2. Find a passage from a text in your field of study and examine it with an eye toward its audience, its presuppositions, and its point of view. Feel free to use this textbook.

3. Examine a passage from a textbook in a field in which your students study. What is the function of the passage and of its subparts? In what ways does the text "announce its membership" in a particular discourse community?

4. Locate a newspaper article that can be used as a good example for distinguishing fact from opinion. Develop a set of questions or activities that you would bring to class to help ESOL students work on ways to distinguish fact from opinion.

5. Locate a newspaper editorial, book review, or other "opinion piece." What distinguishes this kind of writing from less explicit editorializing?

·CHAPTER SIX·
FICTION, POETRY, AND SONGS

A renewed interest in literature and songs in the second language classroom is evident in contemporary teacher-training and classroom texts.[1] As the field rediscovers the utility of nonexpository reading, teachers will need to determine their goals for these texts. It is worth cautioning against the presentation of literature and songs solely as vehicles for teaching literary appreciation; second language students needn't be burdened with the apparatus of literary criticism.

Several characteristics of literature and songs recommend their use in the language classroom. Among them are these suggested by Maley and Duff (1989):

- **Universality:** Literature and music are universal in human cultures.

- **Nontriviality:** Unlike some expository prose, these texts often address fundamental issues of the human condition.

- **Motivation:** The individual responses engendered by literary texts and music can prove motivating in the language classroom as can the pleasure and variety afforded by these texts.

In addition, literature and songs can be used to teach the following elements of a second language:

- **Cultural information:** These texts are particularly suited to teaching elements of the culture that produced them (see, for example, Lach-Newinsky & Seletzky, 1986).

- **Syntactic markers/discourse structure:** Poetry, in particular, can be an effective vehicle for highlighting these aspects of English.

- **Teaching language rhythm:** These written texts can be used to develop a feeling for the rhythm of oral and written English.

In this chapter, we will focus on the use of fiction, poetry, and songs to teach the approaches to reading introduced elsewhere in the curriculum. Students benefit from prereading activities and from reading as part of a task, with a clear purpose in mind. Extensive reading of longer texts can be combined with careful reading of portions of text. In the course of reading and enjoying literature and songs, students can practice recognizing syntactic and discourse clues, recognizing pre-suppositions/drawing inferences, and evaluating texts in terms of their systems of beliefs. We will not address here the details of presenting longer, extended pieces of fiction.[2] As we have already encountered a sample lesson using poetry in Chapter One, we will go directly to specific examples of approaches to literature and music in the ESOL classroom.

READING FOR THE MAIN IDEA

Poetry

The "compactness" (Maley & Duff, 1989) of poetry, in particular, allows students to read an entire (con)text and identify what is often a single major concept. In the example below, students are asked to read simply to identify the object being described.

Southbound on the Freeway

A tourist came in from Orbitville,
parked in the air, and said:

The creatures of this star
are made of metal and glass.

Through the transparent part
you can see their guts.

Their feet are round and roll
on diagrams—or long

measuring tapes—dark
with white lines.

They have four eyes.
The two in the back are red.

Sometimes you can see a 5-eyed
one, with a red eye turning

on the top of his head.
He must be special—

The others respect him,
and go slow

when he passes, winding
among them from behind.
They all hiss as they glide,
like inches, down the marked

tapes. Those soft shapes,
shadowy inside

the hard bodies—are they
their guts or their brains?

*May Swenson**

Fables

Students can also use fables to consider the main idea of a passage. In their familiar capacity as exemplars of cultural values, fables have a seemingly universal appeal. Below is a sample fable for which students can be asked to provide a moral or "main idea."†

> A man once owned a chicken that laid eggs made of gold. But the man did not want to wait patiently for each golden egg to be laid. He wanted all his treasure at once, and so he killed the chicken, thinking that inside her he would find solid gold. Sadly, after cutting open the chicken, he found only flesh and blood.

READING FOR DETAILS

Mystery

Mystery stories present the reader with a problem that is soluble through careful reading. Below is an example from a series of stories about the detective Professor Fordney. The mystery is followed by a single question.

---

*From *Poems to Solve* by May Swenson, New York: Charles Scribner's Sons, 1966.

†From: *Literate Choices* by M.A. Clarke, B.K. Dobson, and S. Silberstein, Ann Arbor, Mich.: University of Michigan Press, forthcoming. Adapted from "Much Wants More," *Tales from Aesop,* by H. Jones, 1981, New York: Franklin Watts.

"I shall tell you," Fordney said to his class some years ago, "of an exploit of the famed scientist, Sir Joshua Beckwith, Professor of Egyptology in London.

"He had uncovered an ancient tomb in Egypt and, through his undisputed knowledge and ability to read hieroglyphics, had definitely established the date of the birth and the reign of a great Pharaoh whose mummy he had discovered. A man who was easily angered, he had many enemies.

"The British Museum soon received a message, signed by Sir Joshua, which in part read as follows: 'Have discovered the tomb of an important Pharaoh who reigned from 1410 to 1428 B.C. and who died at the age of 42 years, leaving two sons and two daughters. Great wealth found. . . . One of his sons died shortly after his reign began, etc. . . .'

"The Museum officials at first were astonished," continued Fordney, "but examination of the communication quickly told them it was either a very stupid fake or an attempt at a 'practical joke'!

"They were right in their belief that the message did not come from Sir Joshua Beckwith. He did make a most important discovery—but how did the Museum authorities know the communication was not authentic?"

*How did they know?**

DRAWING INFERENCES

The following two poems "celebrate" spring. Each requires drawing inferences in order to comprehend the full sense of the poem. As a prereading activity, it proves useful to discuss cultural associations with changing seasons. The ambitious instructor can read the first poem aloud using the stress markings to try to capture what Hopkins called his "sprung rhythm."

Poetry: Using Syntactic and Lexical Clues

Gerard Manley Hopkins's poem begins with a question: Why is Margaret grieving? The poem unfolds to provide an answer.

---

*From: *Minute Mysteries* by Austin Ripley, New York: Pocket Books, 1949.

Spring and Fall:
to a young child

1 Márgarét, áre you grieving
   Over Goldengrove unleaving?
   Léaves, líke the things of man, you
   With your fresh thoughts care for, can you?

5 Áh! ás the heart grows older
   It will come to such sights colder
   By and by, nor spare a sigh
   Though worlds of wanwood leafmeal lie;
   And yet you wíll weep and know why.

10 Now no matter child the name:
    Sórrow's spríngs áre the same.
    Nor mouth had, no nor mind, expressed
    What heart heard of, ghost guessed:
    It ís the blight man was born for,

15 It is Margaret you mourn for.

*Gerard Manley Hopkins **

Students can first untangle the unusual syntax in lines 3–4 and 12–13, converting these to more standard English. The invented words—compounds formed by combining words and/or affixes—are also an important part of the poem. Even if students use their dictionaries to define word parts, they will find themselves using context and their inferencing skills to determine the meanings of these unique combinations:

Goldengrove (line 2)   wanwood (line 8)
unleaving (line 2)   leafmeal (line 8)

Having looked more closely at the language of the poem, students can read it carefully to determine why Margaret is grieving.

Poetry: Using Visual and Lexical Clues

The poet e.e. cummings plays with language. He is noted for his place-ment of words on the page and his unusual use of lower case and capital letters. The poem below requires drawing inferences, in part, on the basis of visual and lexical clues.

---

*From *Poetry: From Statement to Meaning* by J. Beaty and W.H. Matchett, 1965, (p. 62) New York: Oxford University Press.

in Just-

in Just-
spring   when the world is mud-
luscious the little
lame balloonman

whistles   far   and wee

and eddieandbill come
running from marbles and
piracies and it's
spring

when the world is puddle-wonderful

the queer
old balloonman whistles
far   and   wee
and bettyandisabel come dancing

from hop-scotch and jump-rope and

it's
spring
and
    the

        goat-footed

balloonMan   whistles
far
and
wee

e.e. cummings *

Teachers may want to read the poem aloud to demonstrate the effects achieved by the unusual spacing. Like Hopkins, cummings invents words. In this poem, the words *mud-luscious* and *puddle-wonderful* have been created by combining common English words. Students can speculate on the meanings of these terms and evaluate whether they feel that cummings' unusual spacing and invented words are effective.

*From *E.E. Cummings: Complete Poems, 1913–1962*. New York: Harcourt, Brace, Jovanovich, 1980.

Ultimately, the task in reading this poem is to decide for oneself what kind of spring is being described. Is the spirit of the poem happy? sad? threatening? Students use evidence from the poem to debate whether this spring is primarily "in Just" and devilish, or exuberant with children.

DRAWING INFERENCES: PREDICTION

Fiction: Inferring from Details

The passage below is the beginning of a story by Nathaniel Hawthorne. * Students can enjoy predicting what will happen to young Robin next, if they are able to read carefully and draw inferences.

> It was not yet eleven o'clock when a boat crossed the river with a single passenger who had obtained his transportation at that unusual hour by promising an extra fare. While the youth stood on the landing-place searching in his pockets for money, the ferryman lifted his lantern, by the aid of which, together with the newly risen moon, he took a very accurate survey of the stranger's figure. He was a young man of barely eighteen years, evidently country bred, and now, as it seemed, on his first visit to town. He was wearing a rough gray coat, which was in good shape, but which had seen many winters before this one. The garments under his coat were well constructed of leather, and fitted tightly to a pair of muscular legs; his stockings of blue yarn must have been the work of a mother or sister, and on his head was a three-cornered hat, which in its better days had perhaps sheltered the grayer head of the lad's father. In his left hand was a walking stick, and his equipment was completed by a leather bag not so abundantly stocked as to inconvenience the strong shoulders on which it hung. Brown curly hair, well-shaped features, bright, cheerful eyes were nature's gifts, and worth all that art could have done for his adornment. The youth, whose name was Robin, paid the boatman, and then walked forward into town with a light step, as if he had not already traveled more than thirty miles that day. As he walked, he surveyed his surroundings as eagerly as if he were entering London or Madrid, instead of the little metropolis of a New England colony.

In order to determine whether students have fully understood what has transpired in the passage, questions like the following might be posed during a discussion of what students know about Robin:

---

*From *Selected Tales and Sketches* by Nathaniel Hawthorne, (pp. 13–14) (H. Waggoner Hyatt, ed.), 1962, Chicago: Holt Rinehart and Winston.

1. At what time of day did Robin cross the river?
2. Why was the boatman willing to take Robin across?
3. What kind of a family did Robin come from?
4. Where was he from?
5. How far had he traveled?
6. Had Robin been to town before?

Finally, students can use information from the passage and their prior knowledge of fiction and of life to discuss why they think Robin is going to town and what they think will happen to him.

Songs

Songs bridge universality and "culture-boundedness" (Shaw, 1992). Songs on universal topics such as leaving a loved one allow students to recognize what they understand because they are human and what they bring to texts that is specific to their backgrounds. Many second language students are particularly familiar with the kind of leave-taking described in John Denver's "Leaving on a Jet Plane":*

Leaving on a Jet Plane

My bags are packed I'm ready to go
I'm standing here outside your door
I hate to wake you up to say goodbye
But the dawn is breaking it's early morn
The taxi's waiting he's blowing his horn
Already I'm so lonesome I could cry

So kiss me and smile for me
Tell me that you'll wait for me
Hold me like you'll never let me go

'Cause I'm leaving on a jet plane
Don't know when I'll be back again
Oh babe, I hate to go.

Students can speculate on the following issues: What is the relationship of the speaker and listener? Where is the speaker going? What will happen next? What elements of this song seem familiar? strange?

---

*From "Leaving on a Jet Plane" by J. Denver. Copyright 1967 by Cherry Lane Music.

Children's Literature

One can gain considerable insight into a culture by reading its literature
for children. In the children's book, *The Rescuers,* mice rescue prisoners from jails around the world. As an introduction to this reading,
students can explore what things are universal about prisons and prisoners. Here is the opening to the book as adapted for a mid-level ESOL
audience: *

> "Ladies and Gentlemen," cried Madam Chairwoman Mouse, "we now
> come to the most important topic of our meeting! Silence for the Sec-
> retary!"
>   It was a full meeting of the Prisoners' Aid Society. Everyone knows
> that the mice are the prisoner's friends—sharing his dry bread crumbs
> even when they are not hungry. What is less well known is how re-
> markably they are organized. Not a prison in any land but has its own
> national branch of a wonderful, world-wide system.
>   The Secretary rose. Madam Chairwoman sat back in her seat and
> fixed her clever eyes on his graying back. How she would have liked
> to put the matter to the meeting herself! An enterprise so difficult and
> dangerous! Dear, faithful old comrade as the Secretary was, had he the
> necessary eloquence? But rules are rules.

The meeting takes the decision to recruit the beautiful and spoiled
Miss Bianca (the pet mouse of an ambassador's son) to save a prisoner
in the Black Castle. The description of the decision relies heavily on
inferences. This rhetorical strategy lends itself to activities focusing on
restatement and inference. Students check all statements that are re-
statements or inferences following reprinted portions of the passage:

> Madam Chairwoman thought, "Dear, faithful old comrade as the Sec-
> retary was, had he the necessary eloquence? But rules are rules."

_____ a. Madam Chairwoman believes in following rules.

_____ b. Madam Chairwoman is worried that the Secretary is too
           old for his job.

_____ c. Madam Chairwoman is worried that the Secretary cannot
           be eloquent enough.

_____ d. Madam Chairwoman believes that the Secretary must speak
           because of the rules.

---

*From *Literate Choices* by M. A. Clark, B. K. Dobson, and S. Silberstein, forthcoming,
Ann Arbor, Mich.: University of Michigan Press. Passage adapted from *The Rescuers* (pp.
3–4), by S. Sharp, 1957, Boston: Little Brown.

By the end of the first chapter, readers are left with a series of questions, notably: Will Miss Bianca agree to help? Will the prisoner be freed? Integrating reading and writing activities, students can write a version of the next episode, predicting responses to the unresolved questions. Evaluating the story in terms of their own systems of belief, students can explore the implications of the presupposition that all nations have prisoners with whom we should be sympathetic.

CRITICAL READING

Folksong

The longevity of folksongs attests to their success in incorporating core values of a culture. Below is the first stanza of "The Battle Hymn of the Republic." Written during the U.S. Civil War, it became the marching song of the Northern armies. It survives today, one could argue, because it expresses an historically important strain of national consciousness: the notion of divine sponsorship.

The Battle Hymn of the Republic

Mine eyes have seen the glory of the coming of the Lord;
He is trampling out the vintage where the grapes of wrath are
    stored;
He hath loos'd the fateful lightning of His terrible swift sword,
His truth is marching on.

In this song/poem the Lord tramples the grapes that contain his wrath. God's wrath released against their opponents, the singers identify their cause as a divine commission. Reading critically, students can note the contemporary relevance of this nineteenth-century song, and discuss its relevance for them.

Note that one of the reasons for developing critical reading skills is because they are particularly valuable when confronting controversial issues. *As always, teachers will need to exercise judgment and discretion in deciding whether to employ a particular text or topic as a teaching tool with a specific group of students.*

EXTENSIVE READING

Reading large amounts of prose for enjoyment and general comprehension (sometimes termed **sustained silent reading** or **SSR**) can aid in developing both identification and interpretation skills. At appropriate levels, students can appreciate reading simplified texts; "readers" are available from a number of publishers including HarperCollins, Heinle & Heinle, Literacy Volunteers of New York City (Writers' Voices), Longman, Macmillan, Oxford University Press, Prentice Hall Regents, and Scott Foresman. In some reading programs extensive reading is handled through a reading lab.[3] Students sign out one book per week, for example, and write a brief written report. Some curricula allow class time to be set aside for extensive reading. For example, students can spend one class session per week simply reading. **Dialogue journals**[4] in which students and teachers write back and forth sharing reactions to a book can facilitate integration of reading and writing. Another approach is the **double entry** or **dialectical** notebook (Berthoff, 1981) in which students copy passages that have particular significance to them in one column and write their reactions in another. A variation is for students to write reactions to readings in one column and their reflections on these reactions in the other (Zamel, 1992). It is important that journals not be graded or corrected. Extensive reading and free writing require that students read and write without fear of evaluation.

SUMMARY

Literature and songs allow students to practice the same elements of second language reading encountered elsewhere in the curriculum. Additionally, they bring to the language classroom an aesthetic pleasure often unattainable through other reading.

Fiction. Short fiction, in particular, lends itself to use in the second language curriculum. Fiction inspires use of inferencing and prediction skills that serve students well when interpreting expository prose.

Children's literature provides a window into the way cultures attempt to reproduce themselves through their children. Students enjoy reading these texts which are familiar in many ways while simultaneously culturally specific.

Fables and other traditional literature have the advantage of being familiar genres to most readers. Like (other) children's literature, fables seek to capture universal human truths, often placed within a particular cultural perspective. Fables invite cross-cultural comparisons, especially as students work to predict the moral.

Poetry. The "strangeness" of poetry provides students with opportunities to focus on all aspects of reading. As we have seen above and in Chapter One, students read in diverse ways depending on the poem: for a general sense, for detailed understanding, and to evaluate reactions to the text. The precision of poetry highlights the use of syntax and vocabulary.

Songs. Songs are a window on a culture and on cultural history. Folksongs attribute their survival to some aspects of universality while they illuminate particular historical moments. Through music, students encounter the rhythm of a language and infer meaning of vocabulary and concepts from context.

·ACTIVITIES·

1. Locate an example of children's literature in English that would be appropriate for an ESOL class. What prereading activities would be necessary to introduce the text? What elements of its culture or cultural history does the text highlight? In broad terms, what would be the format of activities using this text?

2. What kinds of music do you think would be particularly appropriate in the language classroom? Choose a contemporary or traditional song and develop a brief lesson plan or set of tasks around it.

3. Locate a *short* piece of fiction that you might use in an ESOL class. Make any simplifications you feel would be necessary to bring this into a classroom you have in mind. In broad terms, what would be the format of a class session using this text?

4. See Activity Item 2a in Chapter One.

Notes

[1] For further comments on the use of literature and songs in the second language classroom, see, for example, Brumfit (1985); Brumfit and Carter (1986); Collie and Slater (1987); Dennis (1987); Greenwood (1988); Griffin and Dennis (1979); Lach-Newinsky and Seletzky (1986); Maley and Duff (1989); McRae and Boardman (1984); Sage (1987); Widdowson (1975); and Yorio and Morse (1981).

[2] For useful discussions on presenting extended pieces of fiction, see, for example, Collie and Slater (1987); Greenwood (1988); and Sage (1987).

[3] For a description of setting up a reading lab, see Stoller (1986).

[4] For a discussion of dialogue journals, see Peyton (1990), and Peyton and Reed (1990).

·CHAPTER SEVEN·
DEVELOPING INSTRUCTIONAL MATERIALS

In a variety of circumstances, teachers can find that they will be developing their own second language reading materials. For example, materials are often required to address the special needs of a particular population of students. Below are some general guidelines that are often useful when generating classroom reading activities.

TEXTS

Use Texts that are Realistic in Terms of the Students' Reading Needs and Abilities, and that are Authentic

Reading needs. Look for texts that are consistent with the type(s) of reading students will need to do in English. These may range from technical or academic texts to so-called survival reading of such things as job applications, rental agreements, and residency applications.

Student abilities. Classroom activities should guarantee some measure of success for students. Texts generally work best if they are somewhat challenging, but no more than that; reading activities should demonstrate that students can accomplish something they might not have thought possible. Teachers are usually good judges of the so-called level of a text. A variety of factors can make texts more difficult or easier, including length, syntactic complexity, topic, vocabulary, discourse structure, and, of course, the reader's previous experience with similar texts. Whether to adapt a text to accommodate student ability engages debates on authenticity.

Authenticity. It is possible to get carried away with concerns that edited texts deprive students of authentic reading experiences. Students need to read: They need to read as much as possible, often as quickly as possible, to build up a store of textual knowledge and reading experience. Reading passages should be authentic in the sense that they resemble the "real-world" texts students will encounter and that they require the same approaches to reading. Editing or "simplification" will sometimes be required for the sake of accessibility. Careful adaptation that preserves the essence of text along with the redundancy of natural language provides access to authentic reading that students might not otherwise have.

Of course, careless adaptation can violate authenticity. Presenting students with a simplified menu, for example, does not necessarily allow them to order a meal in a real restaurant. Simplifying texts so that they no longer resemble the original in terms of either syntax, discourse structure, vocabulary, or content violates authenticity. At all proficiency levels, we want students to be engaged with texts that are "authentically" similar to those which represent their reading goals.

The Text Determines What You Do With It

It is dangerous to assume that any text can provide practice in any randomly selected element of the reading process. Telephone books invite scanning for specific information, not careful reading. Technical material requires some careful synthesis, often of prose and nonprose material. Texts written exclusively in the passive voice suggest discussion of its function, *but* only if the passive has impeded comprehension. Texts should be sources of information, not raw material for lessons in syntax or organization. In this sense, all lessons, at all times, should be task based: Readers read for a particular purpose. Texts should reflect the purposes at hand and will suggest the kinds of activities that surround their reading.

READING ACTIVITIES

The following discussion is intended to verge on the paradoxical. Classrooms and curricula encompass competing needs and abilities. To embrace these seemingly contradictory elements of classroom life is to enter fully into the teaching enterprise.

Activities Should Reflect the Needs and Desires of the Students

If your medical students are preparing to study with English language texts, activities can include the kinds of tasks found in a medical curriculum. For example, this may suggest integrating reading and writing activities in the form of lab reports. It does not necessarily suggest reading for literary appreciation, although literary texts may be incorporated into the curriculum.

Remember that a Variety of Reading Texts can Provide Practice in Similar Aspects of Reading

Students manifest not only specific needs, but also broad general abilities and interests. Medical students, for example, might appreciate the opportunity to compare technical texts with essays written by physicians for the layperson and with literature on the same topic. This variety acknowledges students' intellectual breadth, provides a welcome variety, and prepares students for a broader range of future options as readers. If these textual comparisons are placed within the context of discovering the discourse signals specific to individual genres, students have been well served: They have learned to critically examine the functions of text and text markers in general, and have learned about medical texts, in particular.

Reading Activities are Well Placed within the Context of Integrated Language Study

In "real life," reading is often part of a series of activities, including locating texts and presenting material orally and in writing. Even in a designated reading class, activities that include speaking and writing are well motivated.[1] The pitfall to avoid, however, is using reading as grist for a writing mill, that is, using reading tasks only to provide information about which to write. Reading components of any curriculum should focus on helping students to become better readers.

Teach Before You Test

This well-worn maxim remains important. Although students do learn by doing, it is important to try to guarantee students some degree of success. Teachers can model aspects of the reading process and provide instruction in the particulars before asking students to attempt these for the first time. At a minimum, all activities and exercises should contain examples and explanations.

CRITIQUING FORMATS

Listed below are some samples of problematic formats for reading activities.[2] They are presented here to illustrate the process of evaluating
one's own teacher-developed materials; it is not the intent to make
claims about particular formats outside the context of a specific teaching
situation. Each example format is followed by a discussion of its problematic aspects and suggestions for improvement. It is important to
remember, however, that activities are never perfect when first brought
to the classroom; only classroom testing allows refinement of our initial
attempts. New materials have a place in the classroom in spite of their
flaws.

1. Students are gaining practice in reading a train schedule.
Poor: The train to Toronto leaves at

    a. 2:00 p.m.
    b. 4:00 p.m.
    c. 6:00 p.m.
    d. 8:00 p.m.

Problem: Although it sometimes feels that way, life is not a multiple-
choice test. We do not enter a train station with four hypotheses concerning departure times.
Better: Ask an open-ended question such as: When does the train to
Toronto leave?
Better still: Students work together to plan an itinerary using a train
or bus schedule.

2. *Poor:* In the following paragraph underline the word or words that
do not belong. Such words will be of the following types:

    a. illogical connectors
    b. irrelevant facts
    c. redundant information
    d. nonsensical information

Problem: This is an editing, not a reading, task. Students might need
to locate these sorts of things in their own writing, but they do not
often need to read for something that does not belong.
Better: As a critical reading activity, have students read a polemical
text and indicate which elements of the argument are appropriate and
which are not.

3. Students open a reading textbook and encounter a list of questions with the following instructions.

Poor: Below are questions you might ask if you were looking for information in a poetry anthology. Read each question carefully and decide where to look for the answer among the following:

    a. Table of Contents
    b. Text
    c. Author Index
    d. Index of First Lines

Problem: Students were not necessarily interested in, or familiar with, the topic. Moreover, they were given no introduction to these elements of textbooks before being asked to do the task.

Better: Use a student text to introduce elements of surveying before students attempt this on their own.

4. *Poor:* After reading a newspaper article entitled, "April Weather in Ann Arbor" (figure 7.1), students are asked to fill in numerical tables painstakingly designed to summarize all the data in the passage:

Figure 7.1. April Weather in Ann Arbor

April Averages	(Temperature)		April Records	(Temperature)
Daytime High	Nightime Low		High	Low

March	April		Monthly High	Daily High
Temperature			Snow	
	48.2°			

# of Heating Days			Rain	
			6.57 in.	
				1961

From "Outtakes from *Reader's Choice:* Issues in Materials Development," by S. Silberstein, 1987, *TESL Canada Journal, 4*(2), p. 87.

Problem: This task is unrealistic both in terms of students' abilities and their needs in the real world. Students are expected to complete, in a matter of minutes, a task that would require weeks to develop. Moreover, one would not ordinarily read such an article in the detail demanded by this activity.

Better: Present a group of true/false and/or open-ended questions that reflect the information for which such texts are generally read. Here are some examples:

1. Will the weather in April be better than that in March? How do you know?

or

2. T/F The weather in April will be better than it has been in March.
3. What was the average temperature in March?
4. What should be the average temperature in April?
5. T/F Snow is unlikely in April [actually false!].

5. *Poor:* Students are told to outline each paragraph in an article.

Problem: If the purpose of the activity is to aid reading comprehension, it is misplaced. We know neither that students had trouble reading this text, nor that outlining would aid comprehension. As a note-taking activity, problems remain. Outlining is not necessarily the best form of note-taking for every reader. Moreover, we do not know that each paragraph contains enough information of import to the reader/task to repay equal attention. In short, we don't know why this text is being read.

Better: In the context of ongoing tasks and discussions of note-taking, students can be provided practice with a variety of formats; success would be gauged by whether students gleaned enough information to accomplish a specific task, not on the basis of the attractiveness of their notes.

TEACHING VOCABULARY[3]

The issue of vocabulary instruction often arises when adapting texts for the classroom. Authentic texts provide valuable opportunities to teach new vocabulary and to practice approaches to vocabulary building.

Vocabulary from Context

The ability to determine the meaning of vocabulary items from context is one of the most important aspects of successful reading. When bringing reading passages into the classroom, instructors can introduce new vocabulary through use of teacher-developed vocabulary from context formats. Three characteristics qualify a vocabulary item for inclusion in such exercises: If the meaning is not available from the context provided, if the item is likely to impede comprehension, and if the word is frequent enough to be worth teaching, it is a candidate for a vocabulary from context activity.

These activities are valuable in two respects. First, practice inferring meaning from context teaches an important skill. Second, the additional contexts introduced by the teacher will provide semantic links that aid readers in remembering vocabulary items.

Successful vocabulary from context items provide adequate context to suggest meaning without providing a formal definition. It is generally sufficient for students to gain a general sense of an item without its specific parameters. Figure 7.2 contains some examples with explanations to the student:

Figure 7.2. Vocabulary from Context

1. I removed the _____ from the shelf and began to read.

   book
   magazine
   paper
   newspaper

   The number of things that can be taken from a shelf and read is so few that the word *book* probably jumped into your mind at once. Here, the association between the object and the purpose for which it is used is so close that you have very little difficulty guessing the right word.

2. Harvey is a thief; he would _____ the gold from his grandmother's teeth and not feel guilty.

   steal
   take
   rob

   Harvey is a thief. A thief steals. The semicolon (;) indicates that the sentence that follows contains an explanation of the first statement. Further, you know that the definition of *thief* is: a person who steals.

3. Our uncle was a _____, an incurable wanderer who never could stay in one place.

   nomad
   roamer
   traveler
   drifter

   The comma (,) following the blank indicates a phrase in apposition, that is, a word or group of words that could be used as a synonym of the unfamiliar word. The words at the left are all synonyms of *wanderer*.

(continued)

4. Unlike his brother, who is truly a handsome person, Hogartty is quite _____ .	*ugly* *homely* *plain*	Hogartty is the opposite of his brother, and since his brother is handsome, Hogartty must be ugly. The word *unlike* signals the relationship between Hogartty and his brother.
5. The Asian _____ , like other apes, is specially adapted for life in trees.	*gibbon* *monkey* *chimp* *ape*	You probably didn't write *gibbon,* which is the word the author used. Most native speakers wouldn't be familiar with this word either. But since you know that the word is the name of a type of ape, you don't need to know anything else. This is an example of how context can teach you the meaning of unfamiliar words.
6. But surely everyone knows that if you step on an egg, it will _____ .	*break*	You recognized the cause and effect relationship in this sentence. There is only one thing that can happen to an egg when it is stepped on.
7. Tom got a new _____ for his birthday. It is a sports model, red, with white interior and bucket seats.	*car*	The description in the second sentence gave you all the information you needed to guess the word *car.*

From *Reader's Choice* (2nd ed., p. 4) by E.M. Baudoin, E.S. Bober, M.A. Clarke, B.K. Dobson, and S. Silberstein, 1988, Ann Arbor, Mich.: University of Michigan Press.

Although vocabulary from context activities are strengthened by examination of the full discourse context, those exercises designed to teach particular items tend to be written on the sentence level. It is important to remember that each sentence need not perfectly delineate the meaning of the word or phrase in question. Instructors can generate several sentences for a single item to ensure that students will gain a general sense of the term. The first sentence presented might be taken directly from the text. Here is an example:

A cool breeze *rustled* corn stalks in the fields around the town.

The night was perfectly quiet; the only sound that came to us was the occasional *rustling* of the leaves against the house.

The silence of the library was broken only by the *rustling* of paper as people read.

Here is a problematic example of an item using a single sentence:

Poor: A high *priority* should be given to providing public transportation.

Problem: Insufficient context to infer meaning.

Better: A high *priority* should be given to providing public transportation; money for highways is less important.

Clarke and Silberstein (1977) note that the following types of contexts can provide the meaning of an unfamiliar word:*

- **synonym in apposition:** Our uncle was a *nomad,* an incurable wanderer who never could stay in one place.
- **antonym:** While the aunt loved Marty deeply, she absolutely *despised* his twin brother Smarty.
- **cause and effect:** By surrounding the protesters with armed police, and by arresting the leaders of the movement, the rebellion was effectively *quashed.*
- **association between an object and its purpose or use:** The scientist removed the *treatise* from the shelf and began to read.
- **description:** Tom received a new *roadster* for his birthday. It is a sports model, red with white interior and bucket seats, capable of reaching speeds of more than 150 mph.
- **example:** Mary can be quite *gauche;* yesterday she blew her nose on the new linen tablecloth.

Stems and Affixes

Students can also be taught Greek and Latin stems and affixes that supply clues to meaning. This instruction can prove particularly helpful for speakers of non-Indo-European languages. Most of us are familiar with the uncontextualized charts and tables often used to introduce these elements of English. However, activities developed to practice stems and affixes should reflect the fact that knowledge of stems and affixes is rarely sufficient without context to decipher an unfamiliar term. As an example, consider the words *benediction* and *eulogy.* Each is formed by word parts that suggest "saying something good." Only context would indicate that each of these terms is used in a religious setting. It requires additional context to differentiate the two: One is a blessing appropriate to the end of a religious service, the other indicates a speech praising a recently deceased person. Successful practice activities require enough context to make knowledge of stems and affixes useful. One must be careful, however, not to allow the context to provide the full meaning of the item.

1. *Poor:* After the *benediction,* the reception began.

Problem: There is insufficient context for knowledge of stems and affixes alone to help us determine the meaning of the term in question.

---

*From "Toward a Realization of Psycholinguistic Principles in the ESL Reading Class," by M.A. Clarke and S. Silberstein, *Language Learning* 27(1), 1977, pp. 145–6.

Better: After the priest said the *benediction,* the service ended.

2. *Poor:* At Mrs. Cohen's funeral, her son delivered a long *eulogy* praising her many good works.

Problem: The context is sufficiently full that knowledge of stems and affixes is not necessary to determine the meaning of the term in question.

Better: At Mrs. Cohen's funeral, the *eulogy* was delivered by her son.

Although it is possible to create special stem and affix activities like those above, it is often the case that words containing these elements are best practiced in their original contexts. Teachers need only call students' attention to the fact that a combination of knowledge and context can help them decipher these terms.

Dictionary Use

Students often benefit from instruction and practice using a monolingual English dictionary. The elements of a dictionary entry should be introduced before students are asked to use dictionaries independently. Figure 7.3 is a sample introduction from a textbook:

The dictionary is a source of many kinds of information about words. Look at this sample entry carefully; notice how much information the dictionary presents under the word *prefix.*

Figure 7.3. Dictionary Entry for *Prefix*

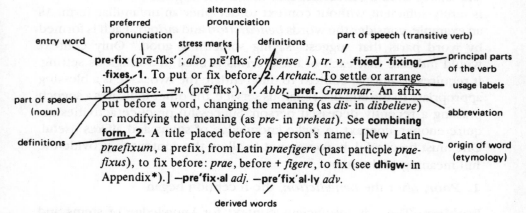

From *Reader's Choice* (2nd ed., p. 6) by E.M. Baudoin, E.S. Bober, M.A. Clarke, B.K. Dobson, and S. Silberstein, Ann Arbor, Mich.: University of Michigan Press,1988. Unedited entry from *The American Heritage Dictionary of the English Language,* 1976, Boston: Houghton Mifflin.

Vocabulary items that are used in an unfamiliar way are good candidates for dictionary practice. Students can learn a new word while practicing finding the appropriate definition in an English-English dictionary. Here are two example items and contexts:*

> We put a *runner* in the hall from the front door to the kitchen.
> The singer walked onto the *runway* in order to get closer to the audience.

Glossing

Glossing is a technique available when bringing passages into the classroom that contain difficult vocabulary that is frankly not worth teaching. A short definition is provided, usually in the form of a footnote or marginal note, or provided orally by the teacher. Low-frequency items that students are not likely to encounter again but that will impede comprehension can be appropriately glossed. This technique can facilitate bringing authentic, unedited texts, such as magazine articles, into the classroom. Before glossing, however, it is important to determine that the item really will impede comprehension. If not, students can be encouraged to sustain the ambiguity of authentic reading.

Sustaining Ambiguity

Even native speakers do not know the meaning of every term in their first language. It is important that students be able to recognize when the meaning of unfamiliar vocabulary does not impede overall reading comprehension. Often a general sense of a term will suffice; for example, within a list of desert creatures, the nonspecialist reader would not need to be familiar with each animal. Knowing what one needs to know is a hallmark of the efficient reader.

SUMMARY

The following are summary guidelines for materials developers.

1. Activities should be realistic in terms of students' reading abilities, their reading goals, and how one reads in the "real world."

2. Reading texts, even those which are edited, can and should be authentic.

---

*From *Reader's Choice* (2nd ed., p. 58) by E.M. Baudoin, E.S. Bober, M.A. Clarke, B.K. Dobson, and S. Silberstein, Ann Arbor, Mich.: University of Michigan Press, 1988.

3. The reading passage determines what you do with it.
4. Reading instruction benefits from a variety of integrated activities.
5. Teach before you test.

·ACTIVITIES·

1. Find a newspaper, magazine, or journal article in English (of about 250 words) that you would adapt for a particular group of students. Edit the text as you deem appropriate. Feel free to leave it unedited.

2. Based on the same article, develop activities that are realistic in the terms discussed above.

3. The passage below is the first paragraph from a magazine article about a course that helps young people make intelligent decisions about marriage.* With a particular group of students in mind, examine the vocabulary presented. Are there items that students are unlikely to know but could guess from context? Are there items for which you would develop vocabulary from context activities? Are there any items you would gloss? Are there difficult items you would ignore?

> The bridegroom, dressed in a blue blazer and brown, suede Adidas sneakers, nervously cleared his throat when his bride, in traditional white, walked down the classroom aisle. As the mock minister led the students—and ten other couples in the room—through the familiar marriage ceremony, the giggles almost drowned him out. But it was no laughing matter. In the next semester, each "couple" would buy a house, have a baby—and get a divorce.

4. Develop two vocabulary from context sentences for each of two words from the magazine article above.

Notes

[1] For a discussion of integrating reading and writing instruction, see p. 70–71 in this volume.

[2] Some of these problematic formats appeared in other forms in Silberstein (1987).

[3] For a comprehensive discussion of the teaching of second language vocabulary, see Allen (1983), *Techniques in Teaching Vocabulary* in this series.

*From "Conjugal Prep," *Newsweek,* June 2, 1975.

·BIBLIOGRAPHY·

Adams, M. J., and Collins, A. "A schema-theoretic view of reading." In *Advances in Discourse Processes* (vol. 2). *New Directions in Discourse Processing*, R. O. Freedle, ed. Norwood, N. J.: Ablex, 1979: 1–22.

Allwright, D., and Bailey, K.M. *Focus on the Language Classroom: An Introduction to Classroom Research for Language Teachers*. New York: Cambridge University Press, 1991.

Belsey, C. *Critical Practice*. New York: Methuen, 1980.

Berthoff, A. E. *The Making of Meaning*. Upper Montclair, N. J.: Boynton-Cook, 1981.

Brumfit, C. J. *Language and Literature Teaching: From Practice to Principle*. Oxford: Pergamon Press, 1985.

Brumfit, C. J., and Carter, R. A., eds. *Literature and Language Teaching*. Oxford: Oxford University Press, 1986.

Carrell, P. L. "Content and formal schemata in ESL reading." *TESOL Quarterly* 21 (3) (1987): 461–81.

Carrell, P. L., and Eisterhold, J. C. "Schema theory and ESL reading pedagogy." *TESOL Quarterly* 17 (4) (1983): 553–73.

Carrell, P. L., Pharis, B. G., and Liberto, J. C. "Metacognitive strategy training in ESL reading." *TESOL Quarterly* 23 (4) (1989): 647–78.

Cicourel, A. *Cognitive Sociology: Language and Meaning in Social Interaction*. New York: Free Press, 1974.

Clarke, M. A., and Silberstein, S. "Toward a realization of psycholinguistic principles in the ESL reading class." *Language Learning* 27 (1) (1977): 135–53.

Clarke, M. A., and Silberstein, S. "Problems, prescriptions, and paradoxes in second language teaching." *TESOL Quarterly* 22 (4), (1988): 685–700.

Clifford, J., and Marcus, G. E. *Writing Culture: The Poetics of Ethnography*. Berkeley: University of California Press, 1986.

Collie, J., and Slater, S. *Literature in the Language Classroom.* Cambridge: Cambridge University Press, 1987.

de Lauretis, T. *Alice Doesn't: Feminism, Semiotics, and Cinema.* Bloomington, Ind.: Indiana University Press, 1984.

Dennis, J. *Experiences Reading Literature.* Cambridge, Mass.: Newbury House, 1987.

Eagleton, T. *The Function of Criticism.* London: Verso, 1984.

Edelsky, C., Altwerger, B., and Flores, B. *Whole Language: What's the Difference?* Portsmouth, N. H.: Heinemann, 1991.

Eskey, D., and Grabe, W. "Interactive models for second language reading: Perspectives on instruction." In *Interactive approaches to second language reading,* P. L. Carrell, J. Devine, and D. Eskey, eds. Cambridge: Cambridge University Press, 1988: 223–238.

Fetterley, J. *The Resisting Reader.* Bloomington, Ind.: Indiana University Press, 1978.

Flynn, E. A., and Patrocinio, P. S. *Gender and Reading: Essays on Reading, Texts, and Contexts.* Baltimore, Md.: Johns Hopkins University Press, 1986.

Gatbonton, E., and Segalowitz, N. "Creative automatization: Principles for promoting fluency within a communicative framework." *TESOL Quarterly* 22 (3) (1988): 473–92.

Goodman, K. S. "Reading: A psycholinguistic guessing game." *Journal of the Reading Specialist* 6 (1) (1967): 126–35.

Goodman, K. S. *What's Whole in Whole Language?* Portsmouth, New Hamp.: Heinemann, 1986.

Grabe, W. "Reassessing the term 'interactive.'" In *Interactive Approaches to Second Language Reading,* P. L. Carrell, J. Devine, and D. Eskey, eds. Cambridge: Cambridge University Press, 1988: 56–70.

Grabe, W. "Current developments in second language reading research." *TESOL Quarterly* 25 (3) (1991): 375–406.

Greenwood, J. *Class Readers.* Oxford: Oxford University Press, 1988.

Grellet, F. *Developing Reading Skills: A Practical Guide to Reading Comprehension Exercises.* Cambridge: Cambridge University Press, 1981.

Griffin, S., and Dennis, J. *Reflections: An Intermediate Reader.* Cambridge, Mass: Newbury House, 1979.

Hanania, E. A. S., and Akhtar, K. "Verb form and rhetorical function in science writing: A study of MS theses in biology, chemistry, and physics." *ESP Journal* 4 (1985): 49–58.

Herman, P. "The effect of repeated readings on reading rate, speech pauses and word recognition accuracy." *Reading Research Quarterly* 20 (1985): 553–65.

Huckin, T. N., and Olsen, L. A. *English for Science and Technology: A Handbook for Nonnative speakers.* New York: McGraw-Hill, 1983.

Huddelston, R. D. *The Sentence in Written English: A Syntactic Study Based on an Analysis of Scientific Texts.* Cambridge: Cambridge University Press, 1971.

Krashen, S. D., and Terrell, T. D. *The Natural Approach.* Oxford: Pergamon Press, 1983.

Lach-Newinsky, P., and Seletzky, M. *Encounters with British and American Culture* (vol. 2). *Working with Poetry.* Bochum, Germany: Kamp, 1986.

Legutke, M. and Thomas, H. *Process and Experience in the Language Classroom.* London: Longman, 1991.

Leki, I. "Twenty-five years of contrastive rhetoric: Text analysis and writing pedagogies." *TESOL Quarterly* 25 (1) (1991): 123–43.

Maley, A., and Duff, A. *The Inward Ear: Poetry in the Language Classroom.* Cambridge: Cambridge University Press, 1989.

McCutcheon, B. *Using the help wanted ads.* Unpublished manuscript. University of Washington, Seattle, 1987.

McRae, J., and Boardman, R. *Reading Between the Lines: Integrated Language and Literature Activities.* Cambridge: Cambridge University Press, 1984.

Minh-ha, T. T. *Women, Native, Other: Writing, Postcoloniality, and Feminism.* Bloomington, Ind.: Indiana University Press, 1989.

Minh-ha, T. T. *When the Moon Waxes Red: Representation, Gender and Cultural Politics.* New York: Routledge, 1991.

Mohan, B. A. *Language and Content.* Reading, Mass.: Addison-Wesley, 1986.

Mulvey, L. *Visual and Other Pleasures.* Bloomington, Ind.: Indiana University Press, 1989.

Nagy, W., and Herman, P. "Breadth and depth of vocabulary knowledge: Implications for acquisition and instruction." In *The Nature of Vocabulary Acquisition.* M. McKeown and M. Curtis, eds. Hillsdale, N.J.: Lawrence Erlbaum, 1987: 19–35.

Nunan, D. "Communicative tasks and the language curriculum." *TESOL Quarterly* 25 (3) 1991: 279–95.

Nunan, D. *Designing Tasks for the Communicative Classroom.* Cambridge: Cambridge University Press, 1989.

Peyton, J. K., ed. *Students and Teachers Writing Together: Perspectives on Journal Writing.* Washington, DC: TESOL, 1990.

Peyton, J. K. and Reed, L. *Dialogue Journal Writing with Nonnative English Speakers: A Handbook for Teachers.* Washington, DC: TESOL, 1990.

Prabhu, N.S. "The dynamics of the language lesson," *TESOL Quarterly* 26 (2) (1992): 225–41.

Rigg, P., "Whole language in TESOL." *TESOL Quarterly* 25 (3) (1991): 521–42.

Rosenblatt, L. *The Reader, the Text, and the Poem.* Carbondale, Ill.: Southern University Press, 1978.

Rumelhart, D. E. "Schemata: The building blocks of cognition." In *Theoretical Issues in Reading Comprehension,* R. J. Spiro, B. C. Bruce, and W. F. Brewer, eds. Hillsdale, N. J.: Lawrence Erlbaum, 1980: 33–35.

Sage, Howard. *Incorporating Literature in ESL Instruction.* Englewood Cliffs, N. J.: Prentice Hall, 1987.

Samuels, J. "The method of repeated readings." *The Reading Teacher* 32 (1979): 403–8.

Shaw, P., "Variation and universality in communicative competence: Coseriu's model." *TESOL Quarterly* 26 (1) (1992): 9–25.

Silberstein, S. *The use of various genre in teaching ESL reading.* Paper presented at the eighth annual TESOL Convention, Denver, Col., March, 1974.

Silberstein, S. "Outtakes from *Reader's choice:* Issues in materials development." *TESL Canada Review* 4 (2) (1987): 82–94.

Smith, F., *Understanding Reading: A Psycholinguistic Analysis of Reading and Learning to Read.* New York: Holt, Rinehart and Winston, 1971.

Stoller, F. "Reading lab: Developing low-level reading skills." In *Teaching Second Language Reading for Academic Purposes,* F. Dubin, D. E. Eskey, and W. Grabe, eds. Reading, Mass.: Addison-Wesley, 1986: 51–76.

Swales, J. "Aspects of article introductions" (Aston ESP Research Rep. No. 1). University of Aston, Birmingham, England, 1981.

Tompkins, J. *Reader-Response Criticism.* Baltimore, Md.: Johns Hopkins University Press, 1980.

Venezky, R. L. (1984). "The history of reading research." In *Handbook of Reading Research,* P. D. Pearson, ed. New York: Longman, 1984.

Widdowson, H. G. "Interpretive procedures and the importance of poetry." Paper delivered at the third Neuchâtel Colloquium in Applied Linguistics, Neuchâtel, Switzerland, May 1974. (Reprinted in H. G. Widdowson, *Stylistics and the Teaching of Literature,* London: Longman, 1975: 153–162.)

Widdowson, H. G. *Stylistics and the Teaching of Literature.* London: Longman, 1975.

Widdowson, H. G. *Explorations in Applied Linguistics.* London: Oxford University Press, 1979.

Yorio, C. A., and Morse, L. A. *Who Did It? A Crime Reader for Students of English.* Englewood Cliffs, N. J.: Prentice Hall, 1981.

Zamel, V. "Writing one's way into reading." *TESOL Quarterly* 26 (3) (1992): 463–85.

·INDEX·

A

Academic material, 24–25, 43–80, 83, 101
Activities, considerations in designing, 12, 102–104
Affixes, stems and, 109–110
Ambiguity, sustaining, 111
Anaphora, 69
Arguments. *See also* Relationship of ideas
deductive vs. inductive, 53–54, 61, 71
evaluation of, 61–62, 80–83, 84, 85–86
structure of, 49–70, 71
Articles
journal, 57–62
scholarly, 44–49
technical, and other technical material, 37, 62–64, 75–80, 101, 102, 103
Authenticity of texts, 101–102, 106, 111
Authorial intent, 9
Automaticity, 7, 12, 13, 37

B

Beginning level. *See* Lower level proficiency
Belief systems, readers', 35–36, 89, 97
Bottom-up processing, 7
classified ads, 24
nonprose texts, 37
Brainstorming, 21, 78
Bus schedules, 19, 38

C

Careful reading, 11, 16–17, 24, 89, 90–91, 102
Cataphora, 69
Cause and effect (rhetorical convention), 56, 61, 63
Charts, 24, 38, 53, 56, 60, 69–70, 71, 109
Childcare agreement. *See* Contracts
Children's literature, 96–97, 98
Chronological order (rhetorical convention), 56, 61, 63
Classification (rhetorical convention), 56, 61, 63
Classified advertisements, 19–24
Cognitive skills (identification and interpretation), 6–7, 98
Comic strips, 30–31, 36, 38
Comparison and contrast (rhetorical convention), 55, 61, 63
Comprehending process, 8, 9, 37, 70–71
Conceptually driven processing. *See* Top-down processing
Content-centered instruction, xv, 7
Content schemata, 8
Context, vocabulary meaning from, 107–109
Contracts, underlying assumptions of
childcare, 83, 87
leases, 83–84, 85, 101
Critical reading, 11
expository prose, 48, 49, 74–87
folksong, 97
materials development, 103, 104
nonprose texts, 33–38

Cultural context, 8, 10, 17, 88
  children's literature, 96, 98
  expository prose, 54
  fables, 90, 98
  nonprose texts, 35–36
  poetry, 11, 89, 91
  songs, 95, 97, 99

D
Data-driven processing. *See* Bottom-
  up processing
Debates, 37, 80, 81, 84, 85, 86, 94
Decision making, instructor, 15–18,
  102–103
Deductive argumentation, 53–54,
  61–71
Definition (rhetorical pattern), 57,
  62–63
Developing instructional material.
  See Instructional material
Diagrams, 24, 31–32, 34, 38, 49, 56,
  70
Dialectical (double entry) notebook,
  98
Dialogue journals, 98
Dictionary use, 110–111
Discourse community, 85–86
Discourse conventions, 43, 45, 49,
  103
Discourse structure, 49, 88, 89. *See
  also* Genre conventions;
  Rhetorical patterns
Discussion section (expository
  prose), 57, 60–61, 62
Double entry (dialectical) notebook,
  98

E
EAP. *See* English for academic
  purposes
Editorials, 74, 85
English for academic purposes
  (EAP), 43–49, 57–70, 74–83
Epigraph, 76, 77, 78
Expectations, reader, 6, 7, 8, 24, 25,
  45, 62. *See also* Hypothesis
  formation; Prediction

Experiential classrooms, xv
Expository prose, 43–73
  critical reading of, 48
  evaluation of arguments in, 61–62
  genre conventions, recognition of,
    49, 57–61, 71
  grammatical/lexical features of, 49,
    62–70, 71
  inductive vs. deductive arguments
    in, 53–54, 61, 71
  outlining, 49, 52, 56, 70, 106
  prediction, 45–47, 49
  prereading, 44–45, 48–49
  previewing, 44–45, 48
  relationships among ideas,
    recognizing, 49–70, 71
  rhetorical patterns, recognition of,
    54–57
  semantic maps, drawing of, 49–52
  synthesis of information from, 48
  writing instruction, integration of,
    70–71
Extensive reading, 7–8, 89, 97–98

F
Fables, 90, 98
Fact, distinguishing opinion from,
  79, 84, 85
Fiction, 88–89, 90–91, 94–95, 96 –
  98
  details, reading for, 90–91
  drawing inferences, 94–95
  main idea, reading for, 90
Folksongs, 97
Food labels (exercise), 28
Formal schemata, 8
Functions of text, 74–77, 78, 84, 85,
  103
Future tense, 63, 64

G
Generalizations, with supporting
  information, 49–54, 60, 61, 71
Genre conventions, recognition of,
  49, 57–61, 71, 103
  discussion section, 60–61, 62
  introduction, 57–58, 62

materials and method section, 59–60, 62
results section, 60, 62
Glossing, 111
Goals, of
reading programs, 12, 68
students, xv, 9, 10, 12, 16, 24, 44, 58, 102, 111
teachers, 10, 17, 71, 88
Grammatical/lexical features (expository prose), 43, 49, 62–70, 71
modal auxiliaries, 65–66
qualification other than modal auxiliaries, 67–68
reference, 68–70
rhetorical markers, 62–63, 88
verbs, 63–65
Graphs, 24, 29–30, 38, 60

H
Help wanted ads, 19–24
Higher level skills, 7
Hypothesis formation, 6, 16, 22, 25, 44. See also Expectations; Prediction

I
Ideology, 77, 86
Inductive argumentation, 53–54, 61, 71
Inferences, drawing, 77–79, 84, 85, 89
children's literature, 96–97
fiction, 94–95, 98
nonprose texts, 33–34, 36, 37
poetry, 91–94
songs, 95
vocabulary from context, 107–109
Instructional materials, developing, 25, 101–113
activities, choice of, 102–103
problematic formats for, 104–106, 108, 109–110
texts, choice of, 97, 101–102
vocabulary, 106–111

Intended audiences, recognizing, 79–80, 84, 85–86
Intent, authorial, 9
Intermediate-level proficiency, 69
Interactive approaches to reading, 6–10, 37
in humanities and humanistic social sciences, 9–10
schema theory and, 7–9, 24, 37
Interpretive processes (procedures), 7, 9, 10, 11
Introduction (expository prose), 57–58, 62, 79

J
Jigsaw reading, 30–31, 32, 53, 60

K
Knowledge-based processing. See Top-down processing

L
Labels, 19, 28, 37
Leases. See Contracts
Lexical clues in poetry, 91–94
Lexical features. See Grammatical/lexical features
Literature. See Fiction; Poetry
Lower level proficiency, 20–24, 48, 49, 53, 83–84
Lower level skills, 6–7

M
Main idea, reading for
expository prose, 52–53
fables, 90
poetry, 89–90
Maps, 38, 40, 42
Materials and method section (expository prose), 57, 59–60, 62
Materials development. See Instructional materials
Menus, use of, 25, 102
Metacognition, 9, 10, 12
Modal auxiliaries, 65–66
Mystery stories, reading for details in, 90–91

N

Nonprose texts, 19–42
    academic material, 19–20, 24–25,
        31–32, 34, 37, 38
    belief systems and, 35–37
    classified advertisements, 19–24
    critical reading of, 33–37
    drawing inferences from, 33–34,
        37
    relationships among ideas,
        recognizing, 30–32, 38
    scanning, 28–30, 102
    skimming, 25–28
    special features of, 37
Note-taking, 106
Notices, 26, 33

O

Opinion, recognition of, 79–86
    fact vs. opinion, 79, 80, 84, 85
    intended audience, 79–80, 84, 85
    lower proficiency levels
        (examples), 83–84
    point of view, 79–87
    presuppositions and inferences,
        77–79, 83, 85, 89
Organization, textual. *See*
    Relationship of ideas
Outlining, 52, 56, 71, 106

P

Passive voice, 11, 65, 102
Poetry, 3–6, 89–94, 99
    comprehension of, 11
    conventions, 9, 10
    drawing inferences, 91–94
    main idea, reading for, 89–90
    schemata, 8, 10
    syntactic and lexical clues in, 91–
        92, 99
    visual and lexical clues in, 92–94
Point of view
    evaluation of, 80–83, 84, 86
    recognizing, 74, 76, 78, 80, 81–
        82, 83, 84, 85–86
Postreading, 51, 52

Prediction, 6, 45–47, 49, 64, 68. *See
    also* Expectations; Hypothesis
    formation
    with fiction, 94–95, 97, 98
Preexisting knowledge, 6, 7, 8, 16,
    24, 34, 37, 38, 49, 80, 95
Prereading, 7, 20–21, 22–24, 25,
    43–45, 48–49, 52, 74–75, 89, 91
Present perfect tense, 63, 64
Present progressive tense, 63, 64
Press conferences, simulated, 85
Presuppositions, recognition of, 74,
    77–79, 81, 83, 84, 85, 89, 97
Previewing (surveying), 43, 44–45,
    48, 49, 105
Previous knowledge. *See* Preexisiting
    knowledge
Prior knowledge. *See* Preexisting
    knowledge
Process texts, 56, 61, 63
Psycholinguistic model of reading, 6

Q

Qualification (expository prose),
    65–68, 71

R

Rapid recognition. *See* Rate building
    and rapid recognition
Rate building and rapid recognition,
    13, 37. *See also* Automaticity
Readers. *See* Simplified texts
Reading lab, 98, 100
Reference devices (expository
    prose), 68–70, 71
Relationships among ideas,
    recognizing
    expository prose, 49–70, 71
    nonprose texts, 30–32, 38
Rental agreement. *See* Contracts
Results section (expository prose),
    57, 60, 62
Rhetorical markers (expository
    prose), 62–63, 71
Rhetorical patterns, recognition of,
    8, 49, 54–57, 71

Rhythm, language, 88
Role of teacher. *See* Teacher, role of
Role plays, 85

S
Scanning, 11, 16
  nonprose texts, 28–30, 102
Schema theory, 7–9, 10, 20–24, 37
Semantic maps, 49–51, 53, 56, 71
Sentence-level reading, 6–7, 44, 47,
  49, 52, 53–54, 58, 63, 67–68, 75–
  79, 85, 107–108
  syntax, 6–7, 11, 12, 62–68, 71,
    91–92, 99, 102
Signs, 19, 25, 26, 33, 37
Simple past tense, 63–64
Simple present tense, 63
Simplified texts, 98, 102
Skimming, 11, 16
  nonprose texts, 25–28
Songs, 88, 89, 99
SSR. *See* Sustained silent reading
Stems and affixes, 109–110
Strategies, reading, 10, 11, 12, 16,
  20
Surveying. *See* Previewing
Survival English, 20–24, 25–26, 37,
  101
Sustained silent reading (SSR), 8,
  97–98
Syntactic clues of poetry, 91–92, 99
Syntax. *See* Sentence-level reading
Synthesis of information, 12, 31, 48,
  49, 102

T
Table of contents, 75–76, 77, 78
Tables, 30, 38, 55, 109
Task-based approach, xv, 83, 103

Teacher. *See* Decision making,
  instructo.
  role of, xv, 10, 20, 22, 25, 83
Technical material. *See* Articles
Tense, verb, 63–65
Text-based processing. *See* Bottom-
  up processing
Textbooks, 19, 24–25, 43, 48, 54
Texts, choice of, 16, 101–102, 111
Thorough comprehension, reading
  for, 11. *See also* Careful reading
  nonprose texts, 30–38
  poetry, 91, 94
Title, 75
Tone, 75
Top-down processing, 7–8
  nonprose texts, 37
  with classified ads, 24
Train schedule, 19, 104

V
Verb forms in expository prose, 63–
  65, 71
Visual clues in poetry, 92–94
Vocabulary, teaching, 21, 22, 25,
  106–111
  from context, 107–109
  dictionary use, 110–111
  glossing, 111
  in poetry, 92–94, 99
  stems and affixes, 109–110
  sustaining ambiguity, 111

W
Whole language, xv
Writing instruction, integration of
  reading instruction with, 25, 70–
  71, 84, 97, 98, 103

DATE DUE